MORE
SIX

FROM THE
VANCOUVER SUN
TEST KITCHEN

O'clock
SOLUTIONS

Copyright © 2002 The Vancouver Sun

Inside illustrations copyright © Michael Knox

All rights reserved. No part of this publication may be
reproduced, stored in a retrieval system, or transmitted in
any form or by any means, electronic, mechanical,
photocopying, recording or otherwise, without the prior
written permission of the publisher.

Published by
Pacific Newspaper Group, A CanWest Company
1 — 200 Granville Street
Vancouver, B.C.
V6C 3N3

Pacific Newspaper Group President and Publisher:
  Dennis Skulsky

National Library of Canada Cataloguing in Publication Data
Phelan, Ruth, 1960 –
  More Six O'Clock Solutions / Ruth Phelan and Brenda Thompson.
  Includes Index.
  ISBN 0-9697356-2-6
  1. Quick and easy cookery.   I. Thompson, Brenda, 1944 –   II. Title.
TX833.5.P43 2002   641.5'55   C2002-911417-9

Design:	Blair Pocock, Fleming Design
Back cover photo:	Peter Battistoni
Home economists:	Brenda Thompson
	Ruth Phelan
Nutritional consultant:	Jean Fremont, RD
Index:	Marial Shea
Editor:	Murray McMillan

Printed and bound in Canada by Webcom Limited

Distributed by: Whitecap Books Ltd.
                351 Lynn Avenue
                North Vancouver, B.C. V7J 2C4

ACKNOWLEDGEMENTS

We have many people to thank for making it possible to produce this encore to the 1995 cookbook Six O'Clock Solutions.

FIRST, OUR THANKS TO THE FANS who loved that book, and told us so in no uncertain terms — in words of praise and in sales. *More Six O'Clock Solutions* was born out of that steady support and belief in the work of The Vancouver Sun Test Kitchen.

Thank you to all who went the extra distance — especially those out of province or outside Canada — to find the book when their local bookstores didn't carry it.

We're deeply grateful to Dennis Skulsky, president of Pacific Newspaper Group and publisher of *The Vancouver Sun*, for his support and enthusiasm for this project, and for honouring the importance of food and cooking in our readers' daily lives.

Neil Reynolds, editor-in-chief of *The Vancouver Sun*, has been very supportive.

We thank Jamie Pitblado, *The Sun's* director of marketing, who in a lean economic climate made room for the project in his budget, and mercifully guided it through the shoals of publishing, printing and promotion.

Thanks also to Shelley Fralic, the newspaper's executive editor, for her valued support and witticisms, which soothed us through the inevitable frustrations.

Special thanks to Mia Stainsby, *The Sun's* restaurant critic, for her advice, ideas and support throughout this project.

Murray McMillan, the newspaper's food editor, helped keep us on an even keel with his sense of humour, then applied his well-honed editing skills to the manuscript. This book wouldn't have become a reality without him.

We would also like to thank:

· The various people from the newsroom and the Pacific Newspaper Group marketing department who lent their palates and opinions on taste panels and provided valuable feedback on recipes. Their frank and astute comments were always helpful.

- Jean Fremont, RD, our nutritional consultant, who tallied the nutrients in every recipe and weighed in with sound advice.

- *Vancouver Sun* photographer Peter Battistoni, who never ceases to amaze us with his beautiful food images. (He shot the back cover photo.)

- Liz Scott and her staff in PNG's desktop services department — in particular, Craig Ferry and Brian Corbett — who performed heroic deeds to keep our temperamental computers working properly.

- Debbie Millward, PNG chief librarian, and staffers Joel Minion, Kate Bird, Margaret Twohig and Sandra Boutilier, for their expertise in conjuring recipes and other vital data from our massive electronic files.

- Marlene Carroll, who cheerfully goes beyond the call of duty in clipping and filing an unending stream of our recipes as they appear in print each Wednesday.

- The marketing and promotion staff: manager Louise Watson, coordinator Lori Fralic, PNG creative director Jim Emerson, artists Karen Griffin and Kieron Byrne, and Marilyn Chepil, who handles cookbook sales at the promotion desk.

- Finally, to all those at Fleming Design, our undying gratitude for their wizardry in taking our work and shaping it into this book.

Ruth Phelan
Brenda Thompson
Vancouver, B.C.
September, 2002

TABLE OF CONTENTS

THE RECIPES

FOREWORD

··

AT THE END OF A HALL in the downtown newsroom where I work, a red door leads into The Vancouver Sun Test Kitchen.

I love taking phone calls from that kitchen, with its glass walls overlooking the harbour. When the phone rings, home economist Ruth Phelan or Brenda Thompson will be on the line, wondering if I could spare the time to taste a dish they're testing. Immediately, I'm there, like Pavlov's dog.

As restaurant critic for *The Vancouver Sun*, my taste buds are promiscuous and they're easily seduced by adventure and momentary trends. But they always find comfort and grounding in the test kitchen. Ruth and Brenda develop recipes for real people in the real world. Their dishes are nutritious, taste delicious, move with the times, look good without doing headstands on the plate, and they're simple to prepare. The food found in these pages has the heartwarming feel of home and nurturing.

Seven years have passed since the first *Six O'Clock Solutions* appeared. It quickly went into second printing, and judging from phone calls, people have been wandering the bookstores looking for hard-to-find copies. Finally, we have a followup, *More Six O'Clock Solutions*, with another crop of quick recipes.

Over the years, I have taste-tested many, many of these dishes during development. When a dish has been less than knee-slappingly good, Ruth and Brenda, bulldogs in aprons, were determined to get it right. Inevitably, they do — before giving it the "Kitchen Tested" stamp of assurance.

More Six O'Clock Solutions is like having a mealtime emergency response team to turn to. Today's average home cook doesn't have the daily luxury of many hours in which to prepare tasty, healthful dishes, which is why all these recipes can be prepared in 30 minutes or less. And each has survived a gauntlet of taste testers. This time around, each recipe comes with a nutritional analysis — a breakdown of calories, fat, protein, carbohydrates, vitamins, minerals and fibre. We've been as vigilant about health as about speed and efficiency. Most of the dishes in this book are everyday family recipes, but that doesn't mean humble and unimpressive. I wouldn't hesitate to serve many of them when entertaining my most discerning guests.

Until 2001, Ruth and Brenda quietly worked their magic for the *The Vancouver Sun*, developing and testing recipes for the newspaper's food pages. They now concentrate their efforts on the wider audience of CanWest Global newspapers across Canada. Their recipes, as their newspaper fans know, are all tried, tested and true. Which is why decades of *Vancouver Sun* recipes are filed away, dog-eared and yellowing, by readers who won't let go of them. (A woman I know used these recipes until they were so ragged, only memory could piece them together. She now photocopies her favourites for a reincarnated life.)

The reason for such remarkable devotion to tested recipes is simple. In the words of long-time faithful readers: "They work." I hate to tell you, but many cookbook recipes don't, leaving readers to blame themselves for being hopeless cooks.

It's a challenge developing 30-minute modern, nutritious, flavourful dishes, but the meals we all want are not out of reach. With careful shopping, time-saving products can help. So can intensely flavoured ingredients — things like sun-dried tomatoes, pesto, top-quality parmesan cheese, dried fruits, prosciutto, chutneys, pancetta and even jams for sweet sauces. When those flavour additions are combined with quick-cooking ingredients like pork chops, pasta and couscous, and handled with fast techniques, the results are worthy of a top-notch bistro anywhere.

When recipes are created, they embody something of the creator, and here you can almost taste the pleasure and passion that motivate Ruth Phelan and Brenda Thompson. I know them well, and while their effort isn't about ego (far from it), it is far more than just a job.

Sophia Loren once said that the most indispensable ingredient in good home cooking is love for those you cook for. *The Vancouver Sun's* kitchen goddesses don't know the individuals they're testing for, but they have a huge respect for the home cooks who rely on them. When you try these recipes, nothing would reward them as much as hearing, once again, those words: "The recipes work."

Mia Stainsby
Vancouver Sun Restaurant Critic
September 2002

A Cook's Guide to the Recipes

Every cookbook has its own approach to ingredients and techniques. Here, in brief form, are the basic rules that guided the preparation of this book. Cooking is an art form — it shouldn't be constraining. But sticking close to these basic ideas will help you make dishes very similar to those five-star recipes created in our test kitchen.

- Read the recipe from start to finish before you begin to cook. Ensure that you have all of the ingredients as well as the necessary equipment. You don't want surprises.

- All recipes use dried pasta unless specified otherwise. We do not specify boiling times for dried pasta because they vary from brand to brand. Please follow the cooking times on the package.

- Use medium-size fruit and vegetables unless specified otherwise.

- One shallot refers to the whole bulb, not just one clove.

- To save time, we often use packaged, ready-to-use greens and other vegetables.

- Parmesan cheese is grated in the kitchen or bought freshly grated at the deli.

- Salt is regular table salt.

- Pepper is freshly ground black pepper.

- Dried herbs are flaked dried leaves, not ground or powdered herbs.

- Lemon and lime juices are freshly squeezed, not shelf-stable bottled juice.

- Home-made stock is always great, but not many of us have time to prepare it. Reconstituted canned condensed broth and ready-to-use broth in cartons are both good options. Another option is reconstituted bottled stock pastes or fresh refrigerated stock pastes.

- When a recipe gives a choice of ingredients, the one listed first is preferred.

- Mushrooms are fresh white cultivated, unless otherwise specified.

- When we call for purchased pizza crust, use the thin prebaked crusts (shells) readily available at supermarkets.

- Butter is salted.

- Milk and yogurt are 2 per cent milk fat (M.F.), unless specified otherwise.

- The conventional oven and barbecue are preheated.

- Cook food uncovered unless specified otherwise.

• "Chicken breast" means a single (half) breast, not a double (whole) breast.

• Use pure sesame oil where called for, not a blend of oils.

• Go ahead and adjust the amount of seasonings to taste. Hot chili paste is a good example — use the amount that pleases your palate.

• We provide brand names for some products that we feel are worth noting because of their specific merits. If you already have favourite brands, use them. Different brands can yield different results, and may make the difference between an excellent dish and a ho-hum one.

• Bones are removed from fish fillets before cooking. To ensure complete removal, lay fillet flat on work surface and gently rub your fingers over the flesh; if you detect a bone, remove it with tweezers.

ABOUT THE NUTRITIONAL ANALYSIS

• Nutritional analysis of the recipes in this book was performed by Jean Fremont, RD, using the PC Nutricom system.

• The nutritional analysis on each page is for the main dish, not sidebar recipes.

• Excellent sources of vitamins and minerals have been identified according to the recommended daily intake set by the Canadian government in the nutrient content claims as outlined in the Guide to Food Labelling and Advertising.

• The analysis is based on the metric weights and measures of ingredients listed in the recipe using:

> · the first ingredient listed where there is a choice (for example, if the recipe says "plain yogurt or sour cream," yogurt is used for the analysis).

> · the smallest quantity of an ingredient when a range is given.

> · the smaller number of servings when there is a range (for example, if the recipe makes four to six servings, the analysis is based on four servings).

• Garnishes or optional ingredients are not included in the analysis, nor are variations.

• It is assumed that visible fat is trimmed from meat before cooking.

PANTRY GUIDE

Shopping lists are never complete, but selecting a few items from each category below will start you on the way to a full-flavoured pantry. These are items that cut down on preparation time, pare cooking time or deliver palate-pleasing intensity.

Time savers *(grocery items that cut down on preparation time)*
- ready-to-use salad greens
- ready-to-use vegetables
- grated cheeses
- pitted kalamata olives
- prebaked pizza crusts
- bottled pasta sauces
- bottled and refrigerated salad dressings
- sweet-and-sour stir-fry sauce
- tzatziki
- jars of roasted sweet (bell) peppers

Oils
- olive oil
- sesame oil
- purchased olive oil flavoured with garlic, hot peppers or rosemary

Mustards *Try these:*
- dijon, grainy and honey dijon

Vinegars *Try these types:*
- apple cider, balsamic (and white balsamic, too), raspberry, and rice-wine, white-wine and sherry vinegars

Sweet seasonings
- jams and jellies (raspberry, blackberry, red currant, hot red pepper)
- orange marmalade
- liquid honey
- pure maple syrup
- fancy molasses

High-intensity accents
- sun-dried tomatoes
- pestos (basil, sun-dried tomato)
- chili paste
- chipotle pepper sauce
- sambal oelek (Indonesian hot pepper sauce)
- soy sauce
- ketjap manis (Indonesian sweet soy sauce)
- black bean garlic sauce
- hoisin sauce
- mirin (sweet Japanese rice wine)
- Asian fish sauce
- curry pastes
- capers
- worcestershire sauce
- fruit chutney
- salsa

Canned goods

- beans (black, navy, red kidney, black soy, mixed beans, chickpeas)
- lentils
- tuna
- salmon
- tomatoes (plain, diced and stewed)
- tomato sauce
- chicken and vegetable broth/stock in cans, cartons or pastes
- marinated artichoke hearts

Other pantry items

- dried pasta (alphabet, broad noodles, cellophane noodles, couscous, medium egg noodles, elbow macaroni, farfalle, fettuccine, fusilli lunghi, gnocchi, oven-ready lasagne noodles, orzo, penne, radiatore, broad stick noodles, rotini, spaghetti, spaghettini)
- dried fruit (apple, apricots, cherries, cranberries, golden raisins)
- dried herbs and spices (basil, chili powder, coriander, cumin, oregano, paprika, pink peppercorns, cayenne pepper, dried crushed hot red pepper, sage, savory, thyme)
- dry bread crumbs
- cornflake crumbs
- quick-cooking polenta
- instant potato flakes

Refrigerated

- pancetta (Italian bacon)
- prosciutto (Italian ham)
- Chinese-style fresh thin egg noodles
- parmesan cheese in blocks, not grated
- unripened soft goat cheese
- yogurt, plain (2 and 10 per cent M.F.)
- sour cream (light and 14 per cent M.F.)
- light mayonnaise
- dijonnaise
- unsweetened apple juice
- fresh ginger
- lemons
- nuts (almonds, pine nuts, hazelnuts, pecans); all best kept in the freezer

CHAPTER ONE

MEAT

*Vegetables are interesting
but lack a sense
of purpose when unaccompanied
by a good cut of meat.*

Fran Lebowitz

Super Supper Soup

Makes 4 to 5 servings

There is no denying commercial canned soups are more convenient than home-made, but they will never compare to the rich, flavourful soups made in your own kitchen. During cold weather, a warming bowl of soup accompanied by thick slices of rustic-style bread makes an inviting meal. Home-made soups need not take hours of preparation. Our lentil-and-kale soup can be made in about 30 minutes by taking advantage of canned lentils and intensely flavourful prosciutto. When buying the prosciutto, ask that it be sliced thin, but not transparently so. Pureeing a portion of the soup gives it extra body.

1	tablespoon (15 mL) olive oil
2	ounces (60 g) sliced prosciutto (Italian ham) or 3 bacon slices, diced
1	onion, chopped
2	garlic cloves, minced
1/8	teaspoon (0.5 mL) dried crushed hot red pepper
2	carrots, diced fine
4	cups (1 L) coarsely chopped stemmed kale (about 6 ounces/170 g kale leaves)
6	cups (1.5 L) chicken stock
1	(540 mL) can lentils, drained and rinsed
1/2	cup (125 mL) chopped fresh Italian (flat-leaf) parsley
1	tablespoon (15 mL) lemon juice
	Salt and pepper

In large heavy saucepan, heat oil over medium-high heat. Add prosciutto, onion, garlic and dried red pepper; saute for 3 minutes. Add carrots and kale; saute for 2 minutes. Add stock and lentils; increase heat to high and bring to a boil. Reduce heat and simmer, partially covered, for 10 minutes or until vegetables are tender.

Remove 3 cups (750 mL) of soup and puree in food processor or blender until smooth. Return pureed soup to saucepan; stir in parsley and lemon juice. Add salt and pepper to taste. ↺

TIPS

- One (540 mL) can of lentils yields about 2 cups (500 mL).

- If you want to save money, cook your own dried lentils. Use 3/4 cup (175 mL) dried brown or green lentils to yield 2 cups (500 mL) cooked. Here's how: Sort lentils, discarding any discoloured ones; rinse and drain. In saucepan, cover lentils with salted water and bring to a boil. Reduce heat and simmer, partially covered, for 25 minutes or until tender. Drain.

- Organic green (or "French" — but not always from France) Le Puy lentils, a tiny variety, hold their shape well when cooked and have a superior flavour.

Per serving:
102 calories, 6.5 g protein, 2.3 g fat, 14.5 g carbohydrate. Excellent source of vitamins A and C. High in fibre.

Speedy Pea Soup with Ham

Makes 4 servings

The average cook seldom has hours to spend simmering a traditional Quebecois pea soup. This quick version starts with canned pea soup, then adds the home-kitchen goodness of fresh carrots, onion, celery and ham. The result is a thoroughly convincing rendition, in a fraction of the time. Add crusty rolls and a memorable cheese, such as oka from Quebec, to make a hearty, delicious supper.

1	tablespoon (15 mL) vegetable oil
2	carrots, diced fine
1	small onion, chopped
1	stalk celery, diced
1	cup (250 mL) diced ham (about 5 ounces/140 g)
2	(796 mL) cans ready-to-serve French-Canadian pea soup
½	cup (125 mL) water
¼	teaspoon (1 mL) dried savory leaves
	Salt and pepper

In large heavy saucepan, heat oil over medium heat. Add carrots, onion and celery; saute for 5 minutes or until vegetables are tender-crisp, stirring occasionally. Add ham, canned soup, water and savory; increase heat to medium-high and heat through. Add salt and pepper to taste.

SUBSTITUTION: Use dried sage or thyme leaves instead of savory leaves, or you can omit the dried herbs altogether.

Per serving:
385 calories, 22.8 g protein, 11.8 g fat, 48.3 g carbohydrate. Excellent source of vitamins A, B6 and thiamin. Excellent source of iron, zinc, magnesium and phosphorus. Very high in fibre.

White and Black (Bean) Soup

Makes 4 servings

If you keep a few cans of assorted beans on your cupboard shelves, the makings of a fast dinner soup are right at hand. One of the keys to making good use of convenience items such as canned beans is to complement them with fresh ingredients. Look at all the good-for-you flavour boosters in this hearty soup: garlic, tomatoes, black beans, navy beans, spinach, herbs. For a vegetarian meal, omit the prosciutto. Serve with store-bought tapenade and baguette slices.

TIME SAVER: Purchase washed, ready-to-use spinach: A 283 gram package yields about 12 cups (3 L) lightly packed.

1	tablespoon (15 mL) vegetable oil
1	onion, chopped
2	garlic cloves, minced
2	ounces (60 g) prosciutto (Italian ham), chopped
4	cups (1 L) chicken stock
1	(398 mL) can diced tomatoes
1	(398 mL) can black beans, drained and rinsed
1	(398 mL) can navy beans, drained and rinsed
4	cups (1 L) lightly packed fresh spinach, chopped coarse
2	tablespoons (30 mL) chopped fresh basil
1	tablespoon (15 mL) chopped fresh oregano
	Dash hot pepper sauce
1	tablespoon (15 mL) lemon juice
	Salt and pepper
	Grated parmesan cheese, optional

In large heavy saucepan, heat oil over medium-high heat. Add onion and garlic; saute for 2 minutes or until onion is almost tender. Add prosciutto and saute for 1 minute.

Add stock and tomatoes; bring to a simmer. Add black beans, navy beans, spinach, basil, oregano and hot pepper sauce; cook for 3 minutes or until spinach is wilted and beans are hot. Stir in lemon juice. Add salt and pepper to taste. Serve sprinkled with parmesan cheese. ○

Per serving:

303 calories, 18.6 g protein, 5.4 g fat, 48.7 g carbohydrate. Excellent source of vitamins A, C, thiamin, niacin and folate. Excellent source of iron, zinc, magnesium and phosphorus. Very high in fibre.

Chunky Sausage and Spinach Stew

Makes 4 servings

Slightly nutty bulgur and spicy Italian sausages unite perfectly in this punchy, flavourful stew. Yellow pepper, tomatoes and spinach add lots more flavour. This is a lovely hot, one-bowl meal for cold weather. This dish calls out for a hearty bread to accompany it — try a chewy sourdough or olive-garlic loaf from your favourite artisan bakery.

1	tablespoon (15 mL) vegetable oil
1	pound (500 g) hot Italian sausages, cut into 1-inch (2.5 cm) pieces
1	onion, chopped
1	yellow bell pepper, cut into thin strips
1	(796 mL) can tomatoes with herbs and spices
½	cup (125 mL) water
¼	cup (50 mL) fine bulgur
2	cups (500 mL) lightly packed fresh baby spinach
	Salt and pepper

In large heavy frypan, heat oil over medium-high heat. Add sausages and onion; saute for 5 minutes or until sausages are browned and onion is tender. Add yellow pepper and saute for 1 minute. Add tomatoes and water; bring to a boil. Add bulgur, reduce heat and simmer for 10 minutes or until bulgur and sausages are cooked. Add spinach and stir until just wilted. Add salt and pepper to taste. ⏱

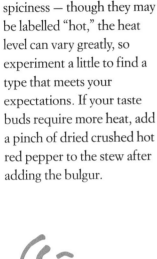

Per serving:
547 calories, 22 g protein, 43.1 g fat, 19.6 g carbohydrate. Excellent source of vitamins A, B6, B12, C, thiamin, niacin and folate. Excellent source of iron, zinc and magnesium.

Lightning Fast Ham 'n' Bean Salad

Makes 4 servings

There's a lot going on in this hefty salad — enough, in fact, to persuade the palate that this is a meal in itself. Lentils, kidney beans, crunchy vegetables, fresh parsley and a dominating note from the julienned ham offer a tumble of flavour and texture. Serve with cheddar cheese bread sticks.

1	(540 mL) can lentils, drained and rinsed
1	(540 mL) can red kidney beans, drained and rinsed
1	stalk celery, sliced thin
1	small red bell pepper, cut into thin strips
⅓	cup (75 mL) finely chopped red onion
¼	cup (50 mL) chopped fresh parsley
2	ounces (60 g) thinly sliced ham, cut into thin strips
½	cup (125 mL) herb vinaigrette (purchased or home-made)
1	large garlic clove, minced
	Salt and pepper
	Lettuce leaves

In large bowl, combine lentils, beans, celery, red pepper, onion, parsley and ham.

Combine vinaigrette and garlic; add to lentil mixture and toss to coat. Add salt and pepper to taste. Place on lettuce-lined serving platter. ↻

Note: We used Maille brand Provencal Vinaigrette with olive oil, garlic and herbs. If using a purchased vinaigrette, taste it first, and add a pinch of brown sugar if you find it too astringent.

If using our Four-Herb Vinaigrette, omit minced garlic from salad.

Per serving:
426 calories, 20.2 g protein, 17.9 g fat, 49 g carbohydrate. Excellent source of vitamin C, thiamin, niacin and folate. Excellent source of iron, magnesium and phosphorus. Very high in fibre.

FOUR-HERB VINAIGRETTE

¼	cup (50 mL) white balsamic vinegar or white wine vinegar
2	teaspoons (10 mL) dijon mustard
½	teaspoon (2 mL) salt
½	teaspoon (2 mL) pepper
2	garlic cloves, minced
1	cup (250 mL) olive oil
1	tablespoon (15 mL) finely chopped fresh basil
1	tablespoon (15 mL) finely chopped fresh chives
2	teaspoons (10 mL) finely chopped fresh Italian (flat-leaf) parsley
½	teaspoon (2 mL) finely chopped fresh tarragon

In small bowl, combine vinegar, mustard, salt, pepper and garlic. Add oil in a slow steady stream, whisking constantly. Whisk in herbs.

Makes about 1⅓ cups (325 mL). You'll only need ½ cup (125 mL) for this bean salad; refrigerate remaining vinaigrette for another use.

The Sun's Basic Burger

Makes 4 servings

GRILLED RED ONIONS

2   red onions
Vegetable oil
Salt and pepper

Cut onions crosswise into ½-inch (1 cm) thick slices. Skewer with toothpicks to hold them together on grill. Brush generously with vegetable oil and sprinkle with salt and pepper.

Place onions on greased barbecue grill and cook for 12 to 15 minutes or until browned and tender, turning often.

Makes 4 servings.

Many pounds of ground beef fed the search for a top-notch basic burger recipe. This is the result — no exotic ingredients that might turn off purists, just a great patty that can let the condiment-crazed go wild with blue cheese, sun-dried tomatoes, tapenade, salsa ... you name it. There's only one rule: Play safe, and cook your burgers until they're no longer pink in the middle. Use raw red onion slices atop the patties, if you prefer your onions sweet, grill them, as suggested at left.

¼	**cup (50 mL) dry bread crumbs**
¼	**cup (50 mL) finely chopped onion**
2	**tablespoons (30 mL) water**
1	**tablespoon (15 mL) dijon mustard**
2	**garlic cloves, minced**
½	**teaspoon (2 mL) salt**
¼	**teaspoon (1 mL) pepper**
1	**pound (500 g) lean ground beef**
4	**hamburger buns, halved and toasted**

In bowl, combine bread crumbs, onion, water, mustard, garlic, salt and pepper. Mix in ground beef and shape into 4 patties, about ¾-inch (2 cm) thick.

Place patties on greased barbecue grill over medium heat and cook for 10 to 12 minutes or until no longer pink inside, turning once. Sandwich in buns. ⟳

Per burger:
458 calories, 28.8 g protein, 21.7 g fat, 35.4 g carbohydrate. Excellent source of vitamin B12 and niacin. Excellent source of iron and zinc.

No-Bake Lasagne

Makes 6 servings

Traditional lasagne usually takes 45 to 50 minutes just to cook, and a lot of time and effort to prepare. Our flavour-packed No-Bake Lasagne stretches our half-hour time limit just a little, but it is an easy version that rivals Mom's. The big difference is that it delivers great taste with minimal work: It's a snap to assemble and cooks quickly on top of the stove. If you keep a box of oven-ready lasagne noodles on your pantry shelf, you can enjoy this favourite any night of the week.

1	tablespoon (15 mL) vegetable oil
1	pound (500 g) lean ground beef
1	onion, chopped
2	garlic cloves, minced
⅛	teaspoon (0.5 mL) dried crushed hot red pepper
1	(700 mL) jar tomato-basil pasta sauce
½	cup (125 mL) water
½	teaspoon (2 mL) salt
¼	teaspoon (1 mL) pepper
8	oven-ready (no boil) lasagne noodles
2	cups (500 mL) grated part-skim mozzarella cheese, divided
2	tablespoons (30 mL) grated parmesan cheese

In 12-inch (30 cm) heavy frypan, heat oil over medium-high heat. Add ground beef, onion, garlic and dried red pepper; saute for 5 minutes or until meat is no longer pink, breaking up with spoon and stirring frequently. Drain off fat.

Add pasta sauce, water, salt and pepper to meat mixture; stir well. Bring to a boil and remove from heat.

Using soup ladle, transfer 3 cups (750 mL) tomato-beef mixture from frypan to bowl and set aside. Spread remaining tomato-beef mixture evenly over bottom of frypan. Top with 4 lasagne noodles, breaking to fit. Spread 1½ cups (375 mL) tomato-beef mixture over noodles. Sprinkle with 1 cup (250 mL) mozzarella cheese.

Add another layer of 4 noodles, breaking to fit. Top with remaining 1½ cups (375 mL) tomato-beef mixture, making sure noodles are completely covered. Sprinkle with remaining 1 cup (250 mL) mozzarella cheese.

Cover frypan with tight-fitting lid and cook over medium-high heat for 1 minute; reduce heat to medium-low and simmer gently for 22 minutes or until noodles are tender.

Sprinkle with parmesan cheese. ◔

TIPS

- Use a heavy bottomed frypan for this recipe and make sure the lasagne stays at a gentle simmer, otherwise the tomato sauce can scorch. The frypan lid must fit tightly to minimize escape of steam during cooking — heavy-duty foil wrapped tightly over the frypan is an excellent alternative.

- We tested our recipe with part-skim mozzarella cheese — at 3 grams less fat per serving compared to regular mozzarella, it's every bit as delicious.

Per serving:

433 calories, 30.3 g protein, 19.6 g fat, 33.8 g carbohydrate. Excellent source of vitamins B6, B12 and niacin. Excellent source of calcium, iron, zinc, magnesium and phosphorus.

Mini Meat Loaves

Makes 4 servings

This mini-version of a '50s icon will taste of childhood if you're a boomer, and if you're not ... well, it's retro and cool.

1	**pound (500 g) lean ground beef**
1	**large egg**
½	**cup (125 mL) dry bread crumbs**
1	**small onion, chopped**
1	**garlic clove, crushed**
6	**tablespoons (90 mL) chili sauce, divided**
1	**teaspoon (5 mL) dijon mustard**
1	**teaspoon (5 mL) salt**
¼	**teaspoon (1 mL) pepper**

In large bowl, combine ground beef, egg, bread crumbs, onion, garlic, 2 tablespoons (30 mL) chili sauce, mustard, salt and pepper; mix thoroughly.

Press an equal portion of meat mixture into each of 8 greased (2¾x1¼-inch/7x3 cm) muffin pans. Brush tops with remaining 4 tablespoons (60 mL) chili sauce. Bake at 400 F (200 C) for 20 minutes or until no longer pink inside. ○

TIP: Use the thickened ketchup-like chili sauce that comes in a 455 mL bottle, not Asian hot chili paste.

Per serving:

381 calories, 27.7 g protein, 20.9 g fat, 19.3 g carbohydrate. Excellent source of vitamin B12 and niacin. Excellent source of iron and zinc.

Grilled Beef Fajitas

Makes 8 fajitas (2 per serving)

Cooking outdoors is all about primitive instincts — lighting fire, the attraction of great aromas coming from the barbecue, eating with our hands. This juicy fajita feeds them all. We tuck delectable slices of grilled marinated flank steak into warmed tortillas along with salsa, shredded lettuce and onions, then dive into a Tex-Mex treat.

¾	pound (350 g) flank steak
¼	cup (50 mL) lime juice
	Vegetable oil
1	teaspoon (5 mL) ground cumin
¼	teaspoon (1 mL) cayenne pepper
½	teaspoon (2 mL) salt
2	garlic cloves, minced
1	red onion, cut into ¼-inch (5 mm) thick slices
	Salt and pepper
8	(8-inch/20 cm) flour tortillas
½	cup (125 mL) medium salsa
2	cups (500 mL) shredded lettuce
	Light sour cream

Put flank steak in shallow baking dish. Whisk together lime juice, 3 tablespoons (45 mL) oil, cumin, cayenne pepper, ½ teaspoon (2 mL) salt and garlic; remove 2 tablespoons (30 mL) marinade and set aside. Pour remaining marinade over steak, turning to coat well. Let steak stand for 10 minutes, turning once.

Brush onion slices lightly with oil. Remove steak from marinade; discard any remaining marinade. Place steak and onion slices on greased barbecue grill over medium-high heat. Grill steak for 8 to 10 minutes or until cooked, brushing with reserved marinade and turning once. Cook onion for 10 minutes, turning occasionally and brushing with oil.

Slice steak across the grain into thin strips. Season with salt and pepper to taste. Cut onion slices in half.

Stack and wrap tortillas in paper towel; microwave on High for 30 to 40 seconds or until heated through.

For each fajita: Put 1 tablespoon (15 mL) salsa in centre of tortilla. Top with ¼ cup (50 mL) lettuce. Place ⅛ of the beef and onion on top of lettuce. Fold bottom of tortilla (side closest to you) up over filling; then fold sides in, overlapping. Top with dollop of sour cream. ○

TIPS

- Tortillas can also be heated in the oven. Stack and wrap tortillas in foil and place in 350 F (180 C) oven until heated through — about 5 minutes.

- When corn is in season, cook cobs on the grill alongside the steak. To grill corn, remove husks completely. Place corn on greased barbecue grill and cook for 10 to 15 minutes or until tender, turning frequently to prevent excess browning.

Per serving:

516 calories, 26.6 g protein, 25.2 g fat, 47.8 g carbohydrate. Excellent source of vitamins B6, B12, thiamin and niacin. Excellent source of iron, zinc and phosphorus.

Beefy Greek Pita Pockets

Makes 4 servings (2 pita halves per serving)

¾ cup (175 mL) grated English cucumber

2 garlic cloves, minced

2 tablespoons (30 mL) chopped fresh mint or dill

¼ teaspoon (1 mL) salt

⅛ teaspoon (0.5 mL) pepper

Pat grated cucumber with paper towel to remove excess moisture. Combine with remaining ingredients in small bowl and stir well.

Makes about 1¼ cups (300 mL).

Picking up a few convenience items on the way home from work is a quick route to dinner with minimal effort. While shopping for the ground beef, amble over to the store's dairy or deli section for some tzatziki — a classic Greek sauce that combines yogurt, cucumber, lemon and garlic. It's the perfect accompaniment to these easy pita bundles, with their Mediterranean flavours.

1 tablespoon (15 mL) vegetable oil

¾ pound (350 g) lean ground beef

1 onion, chopped

2 large garlic cloves, minced

1 cup (250 mL) crumbled feta cheese

¼ cup (50 mL) black or green pitted olives, chopped
   Salt and pepper

4 (7-inch/18 cm) whole-wheat pita breads

4 cups (1 L) torn romaine lettuce

16 thin slices tomatoes

1 small sweet onion, cut in half lengthwise and sliced thin

1 cup (250 mL) purchased tzatziki

In large heavy frypan, heat oil over medium-high heat. Add ground beef, chopped onion and garlic; saute for 3 to 5 minutes or until beef is no longer pink, breaking up with a wooden spoon and stirring frequently. Drain off fat. Stir in feta cheese, olives, and salt and pepper to taste.

Stack and wrap pitas in paper towel; microwave on Medium for 1½ minutes or until warm. Cut pitas in half.

For each pita pocket: Spoon ½ cup (125 mL) lettuce into pita half. Insert 2 tomato slices and ⅛ of the onion slices. Spoon in about ½ cup (125 mL) beef mixture; top with 2 tablespoons (30 mL) tzatziki.

Per serving:
550 calories, 31.3 g protein, 26.9 g fat, 45 g carbohydrate. Excellent source of vitamins B6, B12, thiamin, riboflavin, niacin and folate. Excellent source of iron, zinc and phosphorus.

Cabbage Patch Pork Chops

Makes 4 servings

Pork, cabbage, apples — the classic union in this dish speaks of fall and cool temperatures. Apple juice concentrate pinch-hits for fresh apples and penetrates all the cabbage during cooking. This dish calls for some straight-ahead boiled small potatoes with a sprinkle of chopped chives or parsley.

1	pound (500 g) boneless fast-fry pork chops
	Salt and pepper
2	tablespoons (30 mL) vegetable oil, divided
1	small onion, sliced thin
2	garlic cloves, minced
4	cups (1 L) very finely shredded green cabbage
¾	cup (175 mL) chicken stock
2	tablespoons (30 mL) frozen apple juice concentrate
½	teaspoon (2 mL) dried sage leaves, crushed

Lightly sprinkle pork chops with salt and pepper.

In large heavy frypan, heat 1 tablespoon (15 mL) oil over medium-high heat. Add chops and saute for 3½ minutes or until cooked, turning once. Transfer chops to plate and keep warm.

Add remaining 1 tablespoon (15 mL) oil to frypan and reduce heat to medium. Add onion and garlic to frypan; saute for 1 minute, stirring constantly. Add cabbage and saute for 5 minutes or until cabbage is almost tender, stirring frequently. Stir in stock, apple juice concentrate, sage and any accumulated juices from chops; increase heat to medium-high. Bring to a boil, stirring and scraping browned bits from bottom of pan. Boil for 4 to 6 minutes or until cabbage is tender and almost all the liquid has evaporated, stirring occasionally. Add salt and pepper to taste. Transfer cabbage mixture to serving platter and top with chops. ⟳

TIME SAVER: Packaged shredded cabbage is sold in several degrees of coarseness. Choose the finest shred for this recipe — it will cook faster. In the produce section, look for bags of washed, ready-to-use very finely shredded coleslaw (mostly cabbage with a little shredded carrot): A 454 gram package yields about 12 cups (3 L) lightly packed.

Per serving:
285 calories, 28.6 g protein, 14.3 g fat, 9.8 g carbohydrate. Excellent source of vitamins B6, B12, C, thiamin and niacin. Excellent source of phosphorus and zinc.

EXTRA FAST

Honey Mustard Pork Chops

Makes 4 servings

TIP: If you don't have any honey dijon mustard, use regular dijon and add a touch of honey or brown sugar to taste.

Once you choose fast-fry pork chops as the basis for a meal, you can let your imagination soar — the mild chops marry well with many other tastes. Honey-flavoured dijon-style mustard contributes spicy sweetness to this creamy sauce, reminiscent of a French bistro classic. The addition of cream seems classic French, too, and its effect is to gather the elements into a cohesive whole. Yes, it's a little splurge if you're watching calories carefully, but one that's worth it. Balance the pork with a hearty green — chard, or maybe kale — that has been briefly stir-fried with a little garlic.

1	**pound (500 g) boneless fast-fry pork chops**
	Salt and pepper
1	**tablespoon (15 mL) butter**
1	**tablespoon (15 mL) vegetable oil**
2	**tablespoons (30 mL) finely chopped onion**
½	**cup (125 mL) whipping cream**
1	**tablespoon (15 mL) honey dijon mustard**
2	**teaspoons (10 mL) chopped fresh thyme**

Lightly sprinkle pork chops with salt and pepper.

In large heavy frypan, heat butter and oil over medium-high heat. Add chops and saute for 3½ minutes or until cooked, turning once. Transfer chops to plate and keep warm.

Drain off all but 1 tablespoon (15 mL) fat from frypan. Add onion to frypan and saute for 30 seconds. Reduce heat to low and stir in cream, mustard and thyme. Bring to a boil, stirring constantly. Drain any accumulated juices from chops into cream mixture; stir and heat through. Add salt and pepper to taste. Transfer chops to serving platter. Pour sauce over chops. ○

Per serving:
311 calories, 27.9 g protein, 21.1 g fat, 1.4 g carbohydrate. Excellent source of vitamins B6, B12, thiamin and niacin. Excellent source of phosphorus and zinc.

Pork Chops with Sage and Apricots

Makes 4 servings

Apricots have a short season — they're one of summer's now-you-see-them-now-you-don't delights, so enjoy them while you can. While apricots can seem mild, combining them with hearty meats expands their presence and flatters whatever else is in the dish. That's definitely the case when they're paired with pork. Here a reduction of white balsamic vinegar, brown sugar, sage and the pork jus glazes the amber fruit atop the chops. If fresh apricots aren't in season, don't worry: Look for soft dried apricots, and thinly slice two or three to add to the pan at the same time you add the stock.

1	pound (500 g) boneless fast-fry pork chops
	Salt and pepper
1	tablespoon (15 mL) butter
1	tablespoon (15 mL) vegetable oil
1	tablespoon (15 mL) finely chopped shallot
⅓	cup (75 mL) chicken stock
1	tablespoon (15 mL) white balsamic vinegar
1	tablespoon (15 mL) brown sugar
2	teaspoons (10 mL) finely chopped fresh sage
2	fresh apricots, sliced

Lightly sprinkle pork chops with salt and pepper.

In large heavy frypan, heat butter and oil over medium-high heat. Add chops and saute for 3½ minutes or until cooked, turning once. Transfer chops to plate and keep warm.

Drain off all but 1 tablespoon (15 mL) fat from frypan. Reduce heat to medium and add shallot to frypan; saute for 30 seconds. Add stock and bring to a boil, stirring and scraping browned bits from bottom of pan. Boil for 1 minute or until slightly reduced, stirring occasionally. Reduce heat to medium-low and stir in vinegar, brown sugar, sage, apricots and any accumulated juices from chops; simmer for 2 minutes or until apricots are just heated through. Add salt and pepper to taste. Transfer chops to serving platter. Pour sauce over chops. ○

PORK CHOPS 101

After fast-fry pork chops have been cooked, the basis for a fine simple sauce remains in the pan, ready for the addition of a few ingredients and your imagination. Simply deglaze the pan with a little liquid, incorporating the bits that browned when the chops were cooked. Herbs, dried fruit and other elements expand the flavour palette. These sauces only take a few minutes to make — once you master the basic idea, the possibilities are vast.

TIP: White balsamic vinegar is a light-coloured version of the highly popular Italian specialty, with its deep, subtle flavours. The white variety is mellower, but has its own charm and uses.

Per serving:
235 calories, 27.4 g protein, 11.2 g fat, 5.1 g carbohydrate. Excellent source of vitamins B6, B12, thiamin and niacin. Excellent source of phosphorus and zinc.

Pork Chops with Blackberry-Thyme Sauce

Makes 4 servings

Guests in town midweek? Before you phone for restaurant reservations, consider this: Thin-cut pork chops paired with a sweet-tart blackberry-thyme sauce can be cooked in less than 10 minutes. Anyone who still has plump blackberries in the freezer and home-made jam from last summer's picking can make use of them here. If you don't, the jam and frozen berries can be purchased at the supermarket. Frozen blackberries also come in packages of mixed fruit — you only need ½ cup for this recipe so just pick out the blackberries and save the other fruit for another use. (Take the blackberries out of the freezer as soon as you walk in the door to give them as much thawing time as possible.) Aromatic jasmine rice and tender-crisp asparagus round out the menu well.

1	**pound (500 g) boneless fast-fry pork chops**
	Salt and pepper
1	**tablespoon (15 mL) butter**
1	**tablespoon (15 mL) vegetable oil**
2	**tablespoons (30 mL) chopped shallots**
½	**cup (125 mL) chicken stock**
1	**teaspoon (5 mL) white balsamic vinegar or white wine vinegar**
2	**teaspoons (10 mL) blackberry jam**
1	**teaspoon (5 mL) chopped fresh thyme**
½	**cup (125 mL) fresh or partially thawed, frozen blackberries**

Lightly sprinkle pork chops with salt and pepper.

In large heavy frypan, heat butter and oil over medium-high heat. Add chops and saute for 3½ minutes or until cooked, turning once. Transfer chops to plate and keep warm.

Drain off all but 1 tablespoon (15 mL) fat from frypan. Reduce heat to medium and add shallots to frypan; saute for 30 seconds. Add stock, vinegar, jam, thyme and any accumulated juices from chops; bring to a boil, stirring and scraping browned bits from bottom of pan. Boil for 2 minutes or until slightly reduced, stirring occasionally. Stir in blackberries and heat through. Add salt and pepper to taste. Transfer chops to serving platter. Pour sauce over chops. ⟳

Pork Chops with Red Onion Marmalade

Makes 4 servings

Onions have a remarkable ability to do a quick-turn act: Raw, they can be so pungent they're unpleasant, but with not much cooking, they become sweet and mellow. When red onion is caramelized and cooked with red currant jelly, chicken stock and balsamic vinegar, it makes a wonderful marmalade that plays off pork. Try serving atop a small mound of egg noodles, with steamed carrots on the side.

1	pound (500 g) boneless fast-fry pork chops
	Salt and pepper
1	tablespoon (15 mL) butter
1	tablespoon (15 mL) vegetable oil
4	cups (1 L) thinly sliced red onion
1	tablespoon (15 mL) chopped fresh rosemary
½	cup (125 mL) chicken stock
¼	cup (50 mL) balsamic vinegar
¼	cup (50 mL) red currant jelly
1	teaspoon (5 mL) brown sugar
	Chopped fresh parsley

Lightly sprinkle pork chops with salt and pepper.

In large heavy frypan, heat butter and oil over medium-high heat. Add chops and saute for 3½ minutes or until cooked, turning once. Transfer chops to plate and keep warm.

Drain off all but 1 tablespoon (15 mL) fat from frypan. Add onion and rosemary to frypan; reduce heat to medium and saute for 10 minutes or until golden. Add stock, vinegar, jelly and brown sugar. Increase heat to medium-high and bring to a boil, stirring and scraping browned bits from bottom of pan. Boil for 5 minutes or until juices are slightly thickened, stirring occasionally.

Return chops and any accumulated juices to frypan and heat through. Add salt and pepper to taste. Transfer to serving platter. Sprinkle parsley on top. ♻

TIP: Balsamic vinegar comes in a wide range of quality and prices. A good quality balsamic has a rich dark colour and mellow flavour. Like many wines, the older the vinegar, the more expensive and generally speaking the better the quality. The less expensive balsamic vinegars can be slightly more astringent. To sweeten and mellow their flavour, add a pinch of brown sugar to taste, or simmer gently until slightly syrupy.

Per serving:

324 calories, 29.1 g protein, 11.4 g fat, 26.3 g carbohydrate. Excellent source of vitamins B6, B12, thiamin and niacin. Excellent source of phosphorus and zinc.

Pork Chops with Pear-Thyme Sauce

Makes 4 servings

Tree fruits such as apples, pears, peaches and apricots all pair well with pork. They're combinations where the whole definitely becomes more than the sum of its parts. Combining fast-fry pork chops with the gentle flavour and texture of fresh pears produces a dish worthy of a special occasion, but it's a great family treat anytime. This goes well with steamed broccoli, and buttered noodles sprinkled with poppy seeds.

1	pound (500 g) boneless fast-fry pork chops
	Salt and pepper
1	tablespoon (15 mL) butter
1	tablespoon (15 mL) vegetable oil
¼	cup (50 mL) finely chopped onion
1	firm, ripe pear, peeled and chopped
¼	cup (50 mL) unsweetened apple juice
1	tablespoon (15 mL) apple cider vinegar
½	cup (125 mL) chicken stock
1	teaspoon (5 mL) finely chopped fresh thyme
½	teaspoon (2 mL) liquid honey

Lightly sprinkle pork chops with salt and pepper.

In large heavy frypan, heat butter and oil over medium-high heat. Add chops and saute for 3½ minutes or until cooked, turning once. Transfer chops to plate and keep warm.

Drain off all but 1 tablespoon (15 mL) fat from frypan. Add onion to frypan and saute for 1 minute. Add pear and saute for 1 minute or until onion is tender. Add apple juice and vinegar, stirring and scraping browned bits from bottom of pan. Add stock, thyme, honey and any accumulated juices from chops; reduce heat and simmer for 6 minutes or until slightly thickened, stirring occasionally. Add salt and pepper to taste. Transfer chops to serving platter. Pour sauce over chops. ○

Per serving:
253 calories, 27.5 g protein, 11.3 g fat, 9.6 g carbohydrate. Excellent source of vitamins B6, B12, thiamin and niacin. Excellent source of phosphorus and zinc.

Pork Chops with Red Pepper Sauce

Makes 4 servings

Red pepper jelly can be a secret weapon in a cook's arsenal. It's one of those flavour-packing ingredients that instantly add the kind of intense jolt that turns ordinary dishes into memorable ones. Unadorned, sauteed pork chops can be ho-hum, but when accompanied by a suave, gently spicy sauce, they become company fare. Noodles or rice will work well to sop up the sauce that doesn't cling to the chops. Whichever you choose, start that part of dinner first. Then, because the chops cook quickly, have whatever vegetable you're serving cut and ready to meet the heat, before you start cooking the chops. (Steamed green beans would be especially good.)

1	**pound (500 g) boneless fast-fry pork chops**
	Salt and pepper
1	**tablespoon (15 mL) butter**
1	**tablespoon (15 mL) vegetable oil**
2	**tablespoons (30 mL) finely chopped shallots**
¾	**cup (175 mL) chicken stock**
1	**tablespoon (15 mL) white balsamic vinegar**
2	**tablespoons (30 mL) hot red pepper jelly or to taste**
1	**tablespoon (15 mL) chopped fresh thyme**

Lightly sprinkle pork chops with salt and pepper.

In large heavy frypan, heat butter and oil over medium-high heat. Add chops and saute for 3½ minutes or until cooked, turning once. Transfer chops to plate and keep warm.

Drain off all but 1 tablespoon (15 mL) fat from frypan. Reduce heat to medium and add shallots to frypan; saute for 30 seconds. Add stock and bring to a boil, stirring and scraping browned bits from bottom of pan. Boil for 3 to 5 minutes or until reduced to ½ cup (125 mL), stirring occasionally. Stir in vinegar, pepper jelly and thyme. Return chops and any accumulated juices to frypan and heat through. Add salt and pepper to taste. Transfer to serving platter. ↺

TIP: Little jars of condiments that arrive as well-intended hospitality gifts often end up forgotten in the back corners of the fridge or cupboard. Things like red pepper jelly. As this recipe shows, they can be used to add intense flavour to everyday dishes — a major step up from serving such jelly on crackers with cream cheese.

Whether received as gifts or bought for yourself, these jars are best considered for their flavour-enhancing potential. Once opened, they should be kept refrigerated.

Per serving:

245 calories, 27.3 g protein, 11.1 g fat, 8 g carbohydrate. *Excellent source of vitamins B6, B12, thiamin and niacin. Excellent source of phosphorus and zinc.*

Racy Raspberry Pork Chops

Makes 4 servings

Sounds like you've stumbled on to a dessert page, doesn't it? That's the thing about pork chops — they take well to a sweet and fruity finish. In this case, that means a deglazed sauce that includes strained raspberry jam, raspberry vinegar and chicken stock. If you're serving this during fresh berry season, then by all means, sprinkle some on the plates. A packaged rice pilaf mix makes an easy accompaniment.

¼	cup (50 mL) raspberry jam
1	tablespoon (15 mL) raspberry vinegar
1	pound (500 g) boneless fast-fry pork chops
	Salt and pepper
1	tablespoon (15 mL) butter
1	tablespoon (15 mL) vegetable oil
1	large shallot, chopped fine
⅓	cup (75 mL) chicken stock

Put jam in small glass measuring cup. Microwave on High for 20 to 30 seconds or until melted. Strain to remove seeds. Stir in vinegar and set aside.

Lightly sprinkle pork chops with salt and pepper.

In large heavy frypan, heat butter and oil over medium-high heat. Add chops and saute for 3½ minutes or until cooked, turning once. Transfer chops to plate and keep warm.

Drain off all but 1 tablespoon (15 mL) fat from frypan. Reduce heat to medium and add shallot to frypan; saute for 30 seconds. Add stock and bring to a boil, stirring and scraping browned bits from bottom of pan. Boil for 2 minutes or until slightly reduced, stirring occasionally. Drain any accumulated juices from chops into frypan. Stir in raspberry jam mixture; reduce heat and simmer for 2 to 3 minutes or until slightly thickened. Add salt and pepper to taste. Transfer chops to serving platter. Pour sauce over chops. ○

TIP: The microwave is one of the most useful kitchen tools during rush hour. Use it not only for small tasks, like melting the jam in this recipe, but also in tandem with your stove or barbecue: Defrost, reheat or cook food quickly, maximize juice extraction from lemons and limes, partially cook potatoes (then finish roasting in the oven), warm bread, soften butter. The list is endless.

Per serving:
263 calories, 27.3 g protein, 11.1 g fat, 12.5 g carbohydrate. Excellent source of vitamins B6, B12, thiamin and niacin. Excellent source of phosphorus and zinc.

Pork Tenderloin with Apple-Rosemary Compote

Makes 4 servings

The mantra of modern cooking is Fresh! Fresh! Fresh! So why use dried apples? Dehydrated fruits are an exception to our freshness mania — they have an intensity that fresh versions often don't, and that concentration of flavour is a bonus when you're in a hurry. In this recipe, the dried apples are moistened with apple juice and tweaked with rosemary to add more texture and flavour than would a traditional applesauce. Try these chops with braised cabbage and mashed potatoes (peel and cut potatoes into small cubes so they will cook faster).

½   cup (125 mL) chicken stock
¼   cup (50 mL) unsweetened apple juice
⅓   cup (75 mL) dried apple slices, chopped coarse
1   pound (500 g) pork tenderloin, cut into ½-inch (1 cm) thick slices
     Salt and pepper
1   tablespoon (15 mL) butter
1   tablespoon (15 mL) vegetable oil
1   large shallot, chopped
1   teaspoon (5 mL) chopped fresh rosemary

In glass measure, combine stock, apple juice and dried apples; let stand.

Meanwhile, pound pork tenderloin slices until ¼-inch (5 mm) thick. Lightly sprinkle with salt and pepper.

In large heavy frypan, heat butter and oil over medium-high heat. Add pork and saute for 3 minutes or until cooked, turning once. Transfer pork to plate and keep warm.

Drain fat from frypan. Reduce heat to medium and add shallot to frypan; saute for 30 seconds. Add stock mixture and rosemary; bring to a boil, stirring and scraping browned bits from bottom of pan. Boil for 3 minutes or until slightly thickened, stirring occasionally. Add salt and pepper to taste.

Return pork and any accumulated juices to pan; heat through. Transfer to serving platter. ○

TIP: When pork tenderloins are on sale, pick up several and freeze in a single layer (not touching one another) in large, resealable plastic freezer bags. The night before you're planning to cook a tenderloin, simply remove one from the bag, put on large plate, cover loosely and thaw in the refrigerator overnight.

Per serving:
192 calories, 26.5 g protein, 6.1 g fat, 6.9 g carbohydrate. Excellent source of vitamins B6, B12, thiamin and niacin. Excellent source of phosphorus and zinc.

TIP: Look for rosemary-flavoured olive oil at specialty food shops or Italian delis. Or substitute 3 tablespoons (45 mL) olive oil mixed with 1 tablespoon (15 mL) chopped fresh rosemary.

Grilled Pork Tenderloin with Rosemary and Sun-Dried Tomatoes

Makes 4 servings

Sun-dried tomatoes have the versatility of ketchup, except that they're much more sophisticated. They pack enough punch to transform a pork tenderloin into something special, especially on the outdoor grill. Serve with new potatoes and bright-coloured grilled vegetables.

1   **pound (500 g) pork tenderloin**
     Salt and pepper
3   **tablespoons (45 mL) purchased olive oil flavoured with rosemary**
1   **tablespoon (15 mL) chopped, drained sun-dried tomatoes (packed in oil)**
1   **teaspoon (5 mL) lemon juice**
1   **garlic clove, minced**

Lightly sprinkle pork tenderloin with salt and pepper.

Put rosemary-flavoured olive oil, sun-dried tomatoes, lemon juice, garlic, ¼ teaspoon (1 mL) salt and ⅛ teaspoon (0.5 mL) pepper in blender; process until sun-dried tomatoes are finely chopped.

Brush both sides of pork tenderloin with some of the sun-dried tomato oil mixture; reserve remaining mixture for basting.

Place pork tenderloin on greased barbecue grill over medium-high heat. Close lid and cook for 7 minutes. Turn pork tenderloin and brush with remaining sun-dried tomato-oil mixture. Close lid and cook for 7 minutes or until done. Cut diagonally in slices and place on platter.

Per serving:

233 calories, 26.5 g protein, 13 g fat, 1.4 g carbohydrate. Excellent source of vitamins B6, B12, thiamin and niacin. Excellent source of phosphorus and zinc.

Pork Medallions with Maple-Cranberry Glaze

Makes 4 servings

What could be more Canadian than a dish that combines maple syrup with the tartness of cranberries? Like our national mosaic, it works. Maple syrup contributes a distinctive flavour that's both familiar and a bit luxurious — it's welcome wherever it appears, and these days, that's often far from the breakfast menu. The sweetness of maple syrup and the zesty bite of balsamic vinaigrette play off each other to form a luscious pan sauce. The rest of the dinner is easy — rice to soak up some of the sauce and tender-crisp broccoli.

1	**pound (500 g) pork tenderloin, cut into ½-inch (1 cm) thick slices**
	Salt and pepper
1	**tablespoon (15 mL) butter**
1	**tablespoon (15 mL) vegetable oil**
1	**small onion, chopped fine**
1	**cup (250 mL) chicken stock**
2	**tablespoons (30 mL) purchased balsamic vinaigrette**
1	**tablespoon (15 mL) pure maple syrup or to taste**
¼	**cup (50 mL) dried cranberries**

Pound pork tenderloin slices until ¼-inch (5 mm) thick. Lightly sprinkle with salt and pepper.

In large heavy frypan, heat butter and oil over medium-high heat. Add pork and saute for 3 minutes or until cooked, turning once. Transfer pork to plate and keep warm.

Add onion to frypan and saute for 2 minutes or until tender. Add stock, vinaigrette, maple syrup and cranberries; bring to a boil, stirring and scraping browned bits from bottom of pan. Boil for 3 to 5 minutes or until slightly thickened, stirring occasionally. Add salt and pepper to taste. Return pork and heat through. ⊘

USE THE REAL THING

If maple syrup seems a bit pricey, keep in mind that it takes about 40 litres of maple sap to make 1 litre of syrup. Spend the little extra, if possible, to buy pure maple syrup rather than the less expensive maple-flavoured pancake syrup (which is a combination of flavoured sugar syrup and a small amount of pure maple syrup). The flavour of the real McCoy is vastly superior. Once opened, store maple syrup in the refrigerator. If you buy the syrup in a can, transfer what you don't use to a glass jar and store in the fridge.

TIP: Dried cranberries, a darling of foodies in the 1990s, are often sweetened and can be substituted for most dried fruits, particularly apricots, blueberries, cherries, currants and raisins, depending on what else is in your recipe. Purchase plump dried cranberries in resealable plastic bags for optimum freshness.

Per serving:
269 calories, 26.8 g protein, 13.5 g fat, 9.4 g carbohydrate. Excellent source of vitamins B6, B12, thiamin and niacin. Excellent source of phosphorus and zinc.

Per serving:
233 calories, 26.3 g protein, 12.3 g fat, 3.6 g carbohydrate. Excellent source of vitamins B6, B12, thiamin and niacin. Excellent source of phosphorus and zinc.

Indonesian Pork Tenderloin
Makes 4 servings

Powerful flavours coalesce in this dish, which is anything but subtle. We love the combination, and so did our tasters. It hits all the classic elements: sweet, sour, spicy and salty. But be warned: This recipe squeaks in just under the wire if you're watching our 30-minute time limit for preparation. Plain basmati rice or rice noodles will show off the rollicking flavours. Serve the pork with stir-fried greens.

3	tablespoons (45 mL) vegetable oil, divided
2	tablespoons (30 mL) lemon juice
2	tablespoons (30 mL) soy sauce
2	teaspoons (10 mL) liquid honey
1	garlic clove, minced
1	teaspoon (5 mL) finely grated fresh ginger
½	teaspoon (2 mL) ground coriander
⅛	teaspoon (0.5 mL) pepper
1	pound (500 g) pork tenderloin
	Salt and pepper

Preheat oven to 400 F (200 C).

In shallow baking dish, whisk together 2 tablespoons (30 mL) oil, lemon juice, soy sauce, honey, garlic, ginger, coriander and pepper. Add pork tenderloin, turning to coat well. Let marinate for 10 minutes, turning frequently.

In large heavy frypan, heat remaining 1 tablespoon (15 mL) oil over medium-high heat. Remove pork tenderloin from marinade; reserve marinade. Place tenderloin in frypan and brown on all sides, about 2 minutes. (If frypan isn't large enough, cut tenderloin in half crosswise.)

Transfer tenderloin to baking pan, brush with reserved marinade and place in oven for 15 to 20 minutes or until cooked. Cut tenderloin crosswise into thin slices and place on serving platter. Sprinkle with salt and pepper to taste.

Pork Tenderloin with Tangy Rhubarb Sauce

Makes 4 servings

Every spring, produce bins are piled high with rhubarb stalks destined to join strawberries in a pie, or to become a sweet sauce. While those are laudable uses, rhubarb can play a major role in a meal's main event. Paired with the subtlety of pork, it adds a great burst of flavour to the accompanying sauce. Serve with small new potatoes and crunchy snow peas. You'll need a 500 F oven for this recipe, so remember to turn it on as soon as you walk in the door.

1	**pound (500 g) pork tenderloin**
	Salt and pepper
	Vegetable oil
2	**cups (500 mL) cut rhubarb (1-inch/2.5 cm pieces)**
¼	**cup (50 mL) granulated sugar**
2	**tablespoons (30 mL) water**
½	**teaspoon (2 mL) finely grated fresh ginger**
½	**teaspoon (2 mL) grated orange zest**
½	**cup (125 mL) chicken stock**
¼	**cup (50 mL) raspberry vinegar**

Preheat oven to 500 F (260 C).

Lightly sprinkle pork tenderloin with salt and pepper; lightly brush with oil. Place in 10-inch (25 cm) heavy ovenproof frypan, tucking thin end under for an even thickness. Place in oven for 20 to 25 minutes or until cooked, turning once.

Meanwhile, combine rhubarb, sugar, water, ginger and orange zest in medium-size heavy saucepan. Bring to a boil over medium heat; reduce heat to medium-low and cook for 5 to 7 minutes or until rhubarb is very soft. Set aside.

Remove tenderloin from frypan and place on plate; keep warm.

Put frypan on stove over medium-high heat. Add stock and vinegar; bring to a boil, stirring and scraping browned bits from bottom of pan. Boil for 3 minutes or until liquid is reduced to ¼ cup (50 mL). Add rhubarb mixture and cook for 30 seconds. Pour through a sieve into saucepan, pressing with wooden spoon to extract as much liquid as possible. Drain any accumulated juices from tenderloin into rhubarb sauce.

Cut pork into thin slices and place on serving platter. Drizzle some of the sauce over top. Serve remaining sauce separately. ○

TIPS

- Raspberry vinegar is readily available in stores — gone are the days of having to make your own. You can even find balsamic vinegars seasoned with raspberry juice, but for this fruity pork dish, use just plain raspberry vinegar.

- You'll need about ½ pound (250 g) of rhubarb to yield 2 cups (500 mL) of pieces.

Per serving:
218 calories, 26.9 g protein, 5.5 g fat, 14.2 g carbohydrate. Excellent source of vitamins B6, B12, thiamin and niacin. Excellent source of phosphorus and zinc.

Midweek Sweet-and-Sour Pork Stir-Fry

Makes 4 servings

Stir-fried meals usually take very little time to actually cook, but the minutes saved at the stove are often lost during vegetable and sauce preparation. We took on the challenge of reducing the over-all meal preparation time by scouting out convenient packages of ready-to-use fresh stir-fry vegetables and selecting a bottled stir-fry sauce (one of many now available in supermarkets) – this fine fast pork dish is the result. Simple white rice is the natural accompaniment.

1	**pound (500 g) pork tenderloin, sliced thin**
	Salt and pepper
2	**tablespoons (30 mL) vegetable oil, divided**
1	**small onion, sliced**
2½	**cups (625 mL) small broccoli florets**
1	**cup (250 mL) thinly sliced carrots**
⅓	**cup (75 mL) chicken stock**
1¼	**cups (300 mL) snow peas**
½	**cup (125 mL) purchased sweet-and-sour stir-fry sauce, about**

Lightly sprinkle pork tenderloin slices with salt and pepper.

In large heavy frypan, heat 1 tablespoon (15 mL) oil over medium-high heat. Add pork and onion; stir-fry for 4 minutes or until pork is cooked and onion is tender. With slotted spoon, transfer pork and onion to bowl; set aside.

Add remaining 1 tablespoon (15 mL) oil to frypan. Add broccoli and carrots; stir-fry for 1 minute. Add stock and reduce heat to medium; cover and cook for 1 minute. Stir in snow peas; cover and cook for 2 minutes or until vegetables are tender-crisp.

Return pork and any accumulated juices to frypan; stir in sweet-and-sour sauce and heat through. Transfer to serving platter. ↻

TIP: Bottled sweet-and-sour sauces vary greatly in flavour and consistency. We used Great Impressions brand, which is thinner and milder than some others. Finding one that suits your own taste is a matter of trial and error; dilute with a little chicken stock if necessary.

TIME SAVER: Purchase washed, ready-to-use broccoli stir-fry vegetables (small broccoli florets, thinly sliced carrots and snow peas): A 340 gram package yields about 5 cups (1.25 L).

Per serving:
285 calories, 29.7 g protein, 10.4 g fat, 18.8 g carbohydrate. Excellent source of vitamins A, B6, B12, C, thiamin, riboflavin, niacin and folate. Excellent source of iron, zinc and phosphorus.

Grilled Sausage Burger with Roasted Peppers

Makes 4 servings

The appeal of grilled sausages takes us off the beaten track in our quest for a great burger, but it's a delicious detour. When you substitute hot Italian sausages for the usual beef patties, add grilled red peppers and red onion, then top it all with sauerkraut, the result is one big, bold burger. In warm weather, this cries out for micro-brewed beer to cool it all down.

3	tablespoons (45 mL) olive oil
2	tablespoons (30 mL) balsamic vinegar
4	slices red onion, about ½-inch (1 cm) thick
2	small red bell peppers, cut into quarters
4	Portuguese or other large buns, split lengthwise
	Purchased olive oil flavoured with garlic
4	hot Italian sausages
	Salt and pepper
	Dijonnaise
	Sauerkraut, optional

In small bowl, whisk together 3 tablespoons (45 mL) olive oil and vinegar. Brush onion slices and red pepper pieces with some of the oil-vinegar mixture.

Brush cut surfaces of buns with garlic oil. With tip of sharp knife, prick sausages several times.

Place onion, red pepper and sausages on greased barbecue grill over medium-high heat. Cook, turning occasionally, for 12 to 15 minutes or until vegetables are tender and sausages are almost cooked, brushing vegetables occasionally with remaining oil-vinegar mixture. Remove vegetables and sausages from grill.

Cut sausages in half lengthwise. Put buns and sausages, cut side down, on grill for 1 to 2 minutes or until buns are lightly browned and sausages are completely cooked.

Peel red peppers and place on plate with onions; sprinkle lightly with salt and pepper. Spread cut sides of buns with dijonnaise.

For each burger: Layer ¼ of the sausage, onion, sauerkraut and red pepper on bottom half of bun. Cover with the top half of bun. ○

TIP: Dijonnaise is a handy, creamy blend of mustard and mayonnaise. If you don't have it, stir ½ teaspoon (2 mL) dijon mustard (or to taste) into 1 tablespoon (15 mL) mayonnaise.

Per serving:
469 calories, 12.4 g protein, 31.4 g fat, 34.2 g carbohydrate. Excellent source of vitamins A and C.

Parmesan Polenta with Sausage Ragu

Makes 4 servings

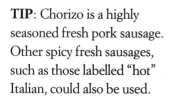

TIP: Chorizo is a highly seasoned fresh pork sausage. Other spicy fresh sausages, such as those labelled "hot" Italian, could also be used.

Per serving:
520 calories, 30.7 g protein, 28.9 g fat, 34.6 g carbohydrate. Excellent source of vitamins B6, B12, C, thiamin and niacin. Excellent source of phosphorus and zinc.

Minute-miser ingredients and fast appliances team up to make this a speedy midweek main course. Polenta can look like cooked cream of wheat, but its base is actually cornmeal, so it's yellow. The quick-cooking variety does just what the name says — when prepared in the microwave or on top of the stove, the speed is unbeatable. The classic flavours of parmesan and fresh basil enliven the polenta, and the spicy sausage ragu speaks for itself — with gusto!

Ragu

1	tablespoon (15 mL) vegetable oil
¾	pound (350 g) fresh chorizo sausages, cut into ¼-inch (5 mm) thick slices
1	onion, chopped
2	garlic cloves, minced
2	cups (500 mL) sliced mushrooms (6 ounces/170 g)
1	red bell pepper, chopped
1	(540 mL) can tomatoes (undrained), chopped
¼	cup (50 mL) chopped fresh parsley
	Salt and pepper

Polenta

3½	cups (875 mL) water
1	teaspoon (5 mL) salt
1	cup (250 mL) quick-cooking polenta
½	cup (125 mL) grated parmesan cheese
3	tablespoons (45 mL) chopped fresh basil

Ragu: In large heavy frypan, heat oil over medium-high heat. Add sausages and saute for 4 minutes or until cooked. With slotted spoon, transfer sausages to plate and set aside.

Polenta: Put water and salt in large microwaveable bowl; microwave on High for 5 minutes or until boiling. Stir in polenta and microwave for 4½ minutes, whisking every 2 minutes. Stir in parmesan cheese and basil.

Meanwhile, finish cooking ragu. Add onion and garlic to same frypan; saute for 2 minutes. Add mushrooms and red pepper; saute for 3 minutes or until vegetables are tender. Stir in tomatoes and simmer for 3 minutes or until slightly thickened. Stir in parsley and sausage; heat through. Add salt and pepper to taste. Serve over polenta. ⏱

Fast Old-Fashioned Saucy Beans

Makes 4 servings

Remember the days when baked beans took eight hours to slowly cook in the oven? Well, here's our fast version, simmered on top of the stove in just 15 minutes. Good old-fashioned flavour for modern times. Add a spinach salad spiked with toasted almonds and a crusty loaf of sourdough bread, and dinner's ready.

1	**tablespoon (15 mL) vegetable oil**
1	**onion, chopped**
2	**ounces (60 g) sliced Black Forest ham, chopped (about ⅓ cup/75 mL)**
3	**(398 mL) cans navy beans, drained and rinsed**
¼	**cup (50 mL) ketchup**
¼	**cup (50 mL) fancy molasses**
3	**tablespoons (45 mL) pure maple syrup**
¾	**teaspoon (4 mL) dry mustard**
	Salt and pepper

In large heavy saucepan, heat oil over medium-high heat. Add onion and saute for 2 minutes. Add ham and saute for 1 minute or until onion is tender. Remove saucepan from heat and reduce heat to medium-low.

Add beans, ketchup, molasses, maple syrup, mustard, ½ teaspoon (2 mL) salt and ¼ teaspoon (1 mL) pepper to onion mixture; stir until well blended. Return to heat and cook, covered, for 10 minutes or until hot, stirring frequently. Add salt and pepper to taste. (If you prefer a thinner sauce, stir in a small amount of water.) ◌

TIPS

• For a vegetarian meal, omit the ham.

• If you prefer to soak and cook your own navy beans, you'll need about 2 cups (500 mL) dried beans to yield 4½ cups (1.125 L) cooked — equal to about 3 (398 mL) cans navy beans.

Per serving:
418 calories, 20.3 g protein, 5.3 g fat, 75.3 g carbohydrate. Excellent source of thiamin, niacin and folate. Excellent source of iron, zinc, magnesium and phosphorus. Very high in fibre.

Fajitas with Back Bacon, Red Pepper and Snow Peas

Makes 8 fajitas (2 per serving)

WHAT IS BACK BACON?

In the U.S. they call it Canadian bacon, but at home we know it as back bacon — or peameal bacon when coated with cornmeal. This lean smoked pork is cut from the tender eye of the loin and is closer to ham than to regular bacon.

TIP: Tortillas can also be heated in the oven. Stack and wrap tortillas in foil and place in 350 F (180 C) oven until heated through — about 5 minutes.

Per serving:
425 calories, 20.8 g protein, 17.5 g fat, 48.4 g carbohydrate. Excellent source of thiamin and niacin. Excellent source of iron and phosphorus. High in fibre.

Ready-to-heat tortillas are one of the quick cook's best friends. They keep well in the fridge and can accommodate any number of fillings. Here we use back bacon for substance, then add bell pepper, snow peas and lettuce for vegetable crunch. The flavour secret is honey mustard, spread on the tortillas just before they're filled.

Kids will love this hand-held meal. Make it even more fun by putting out some sour cream, guacamole or salsa for them to spoon on to their fajita. They might even be grateful for tacos to go with it. A pile of paper napkins is essential!

2	tablespoons (30 mL) vegetable oil, divided
½	pound (250 g) thinly sliced back bacon, cut into ¼-inch (5 mm) strips
1	small red onion, cut into thin wedges
1	garlic clove, minced
1	small red bell pepper, cut into thin strips
¼	pound (125 g) snow peas, trimmed and halved
	Salt and pepper
8	(8-inch/20 cm) flour tortillas
	Honey mustard
2	cups (500 mL) shredded lettuce

In large heavy frypan, heat 1 tablespoon (15 mL) oil over medium-high heat. Add bacon and saute for 3 minutes. Transfer bacon to plate and set aside.

Add remaining 1 tablespoon (15 mL) oil to frypan. Add onion and garlic; saute for 3 minutes. Add red pepper and snow peas; saute for 4 to 5 minutes or until vegetables are tender-crisp. Return bacon to frypan and heat through. Add salt and pepper to taste.

Stack and wrap tortillas in paper towel; microwave on High for 30 to 40 seconds or until heated through.

For each fajita: Lightly spread mustard over tortilla. Place ¼ cup (50 mL) lettuce in centre of tortilla and top with an ⅛ of the bacon mixture. Fold bottom of tortilla (side closest to you) up over the filling; then fold sides in, overlapping. ↻

Baby Spinach and Pancetta Frittata

Makes 4 servings

This simple egg dish makes a comforting midweek dinner, or it could be served for a weekend brunch. At either meal, all you need is a salad and a basket of warm rolls to make it complete. If there's a jar of home-made chili sauce in your pantry, it would be a fine accompaniment.

8	large eggs
2	tablespoons (30 mL) water
¼	teaspoon (1 mL) pepper
1	tablespoon (15 mL) vegetable oil
1	small onion, chopped
2	ounces (60 g) pancetta (Italian bacon), chopped
1	garlic clove, crushed
4	cups (1 L) lightly packed fresh baby spinach, chopped coarse
¼	cup (50 mL) grated parmesan cheese

Preheat broiler.

In large bowl, whisk together eggs, water and pepper until frothy; set aside.

In 10-inch (25 cm) heavy ovenproof frypan, heat oil over medium heat. Add onion, pancetta and garlic; saute for 4 minutes or until onion is tender. Stir in spinach; cook for 30 seconds or until just wilted. Spread mixture evenly over bottom of frypan. Reduce heat to medium-low and remove frypan from heat.

Pour egg mixture into frypan over spinach mixture. Return frypan to heat and cook for 5 to 7 minutes or until frittata is almost set, lifting edges of frittata and tilting pan occasionally to allow uncooked egg to run underneath.

Sprinkle frittata with parmesan cheese and broil for 1 to 2 minutes or until top is puffy and golden. Cut into wedges and serve.

TIME SAVER: Purchase washed, ready-to-use fresh baby spinach: A 170 gram package yields about 8 cups (2 L) lightly packed.

SUBSTITUTION: Use 2 slices of regular bacon instead of pancetta. Cook bacon until almost crisp; drain off excess fat.

Per serving:
309 calories, 17.7 g protein, 23.9 g fat, 5.7 g carbohydrate. Excellent source of vitamins A, B12, niacin and folate.

The Ultimate Grilled Cheese Sandwich
Makes 4 servings

Remember how good and greasy grilled cheese sandwiches used to be? Hot out of the skillet, oozing with processed cheese, the buttery sandwich got dabbed into a glob of ketchup. Today's version can be equally good, just a little more sophisticated, made with sourdough bread and mayonnaise.

If you think it's odd to spread mayonnaise on the grilling surfaces of the bread, the logic lies in the oil and eggs in the mayo. The result is a well-browned, flavourful, crisp surface to crunch into. For a full meal, add a simple salad or soup.

8	slices bacon
8	slices sourdough bread (½-inch/1 cm thick)
8	thin slices light swiss cheese
16	thin slices plum tomato (2 large tomatoes)
1	cup (250 mL) thinly sliced sweet onion
	Salt and pepper
4	tablespoons (60 mL) light mayonnaise

In large heavy frypan over medium heat, cook bacon for 6 minutes or until brown and crisp, turning occasionally. Transfer bacon to paper towels and drain. Discard fat from frypan. Wipe out frypan with paper towel.

Place 4 bread slices on work surface. Place 1 cheese slice on each bread slice; top each with 4 tomato slices, ¼ cup (50 mL) onion and 2 cooked bacon slices, breaking into pieces to fit. Sprinkle with salt and pepper to taste. Place 1 cheese slice on top of each. Top sandwiches with remaining bread slices then spread ½ tablespoon (7 mL) mayonnaise over top of each sandwich.

Cook 2 sandwiches at a time, mayonnaise side down, in frypan over medium-low heat for 3 minutes or until bottom is golden, occasionally pressing with back of spatula. Spread top of each sandwich with ½ tablespoon (7 mL) mayonnaise; turn sandwiches over and cook for 3 to 4 minutes or until golden on bottom. Transfer to plate and keep warm. Cut sandwiches in half and serve. ⟳

TIME SAVER: Buy precooked bacon and warm it according to package directions before adding to sandwich. After opening the sealed pouch, refrigerate any unused bacon. Precooked bacon, although more expensive, saves you time in both reheating and clean-up.

TIP: To reduce meal preparation time, use 2 frypans to cook sandwiches.

Per serving:
315 calories, 19.1 g protein, 15.5 g fat, 24.8 g carbohydrate. Excellent source of vitamin B12 and niacin. Excellent source of calcium, phosphorus and zinc.

Warm Muffulettas

Makes 4 servings

Sink your teeth into these irresistible, enormous sandwiches — our adaptation of an old New Orleans specialty. Simply create a dugout in each little loaf, add the fillings, then finally wrap the halves together nice and tight. Once in the oven, provolone and cheddar cheeses melt over the meat, arugula adds a peppery zing, and pesto delivers the sweetness of basil. Serve with coleslaw.

4	**large crusty rolls**
½	**cup (125 mL) basil pesto**
¼	**pound (125 g) thinly sliced roast turkey**
¼	**pound (125 g) thinly sliced Black Forest ham**
8	**thin slices light provolone cheese**
1	**cup (250 mL) bottled roasted sweet (bell) peppers**
1	**small onion, sliced thin**
8	**thin slices white cheddar cheese**
16	**arugula leaves**

Slice rolls in half horizontally. Pull out some of the interior of each bottom half, leaving shell about ¾-inch (2 cm) thick. Spread 1 tablespoon (15 mL) pesto on cut side of each roll half; set aside.

For each sandwich: On bottom half of roll, layer ¼ of the turkey, ham, provolone cheese, roasted peppers, onion, cheddar cheese and arugula leaves. Cover with top half of roll, pressing together. Wrap sandwich in foil.

Bake at 350 F (180 C) for 15 to 18 minutes or until cheese melts. ⏲

TIP: If you prefer, roast your own bell peppers: Place peppers on baking sheet and broil for 20 to 25 minutes or until skins are lightly charred, turning occasionally. Immediately place peppers in bowl and cover tightly with plastic wrap; let stand for 20 minutes. Peel, seed and devein peppers; cut into large pieces. You'll need about 3 roasted red bell peppers to yield 1 cup (250 mL).

Per serving:
663 calories, 46 g protein, 38.4 g fat, 31.5 g carbohydrate. Excellent source of vitamins B6, B12, thiamin, riboflavin and niacin. Excellent source of calcium, phosphorus and zinc.

Lamb Burgers with Cilantro-Mint Sauce

Makes 4 servings

Say "burger" and most people think "beef." But why stop there? Carefully handled, a wide range of ground meats can be seasoned and formed into patties that provide a delicious change of pace at meal time. Lamb works particularly well — especially when seasoned and garnished with flavours of the eastern Mediterranean, as we do with these burgers.

TIP: If you prefer warm pita bread, stack and wrap pitas in paper towel; microwave on Medium for 1½ minutes or until warm. Alternatively, stack and wrap pitas in foil and place in 350 F (180 C) oven until heated through — about 5 minutes.

Burgers

1	pound (500 g) ground lamb
2	tablespoons (30 mL) dry bread crumbs
1	tablespoon (15 mL) water
¼	cup (50 mL) finely chopped onion
1	garlic clove, minced
¾	teaspoon (4 mL) salt
¼	teaspoon (1 mL) pepper
¼	teaspoon (1 mL) ground cumin
4	(7-inch/18 cm) pita breads
	Sliced tomato
	Shredded lettuce

Yogurt herb sauce

½	cup (125 mL) plain yogurt
2	tablespoons (30 mL) chopped fresh mint or to taste
1	tablespoon (15 mL) chopped fresh cilantro
	Salt and pepper

Burgers: In medium bowl, combine ground lamb, bread crumbs, water, onion, garlic, salt, pepper and cumin. Shape into 4 patties, about ½-inch (1 cm) thick. Place patties on greased broiler pan and broil for 10 minutes or until cooked, turning once.

Meanwhile, prepare yogurt herb sauce: In small bowl, combine yogurt, mint, cilantro, and salt and pepper to taste.

For each burger: Cut about ⅓ off top of pita bread. Place patty in pita bread with tomato and lettuce; top with about 2 tablespoons (30 mL) yogurt herb sauce. ⟳

Per serving:
574 calories, 29.5 g protein, 30.9 g fat, 42.6 g carbohydrate. Excellent source of vitamin B12, thiamin, riboflavin, niacin and folate. Excellent source of iron, zinc and phosphorus.

YOGURT

Spaghetti Squash with Lamb, Spinach and Feta

Makes 4 servings

Inside an outwardly unimpressive winter squash can lie oodles of noodles — not the familiar wheat-based pasta, but long strands of vegetable that twirl apart easily once the squash is cooked. While the spaghetti squash is cooking, put the sauce together. If you'd like this to be a vegetarian meal, just leave the lamb out of the sauce — with the feta cheese and spinach, you won't miss it. On the side, serve a salad of cucumber, radish and mint.

1	(3-pound/1.5 kg) spaghetti squash
8	cups (2 L) lightly packed fresh spinach
1	tablespoon (15 mL) butter
1	tablespoon (15 mL) olive oil
½	cup (125 mL) chopped onion
2	garlic cloves, minced
½	pound (250 g) ground lamb
½	cup (125 mL) crumbled feta cheese
1½	teaspoons (7 mL) chopped fresh oregano
	Salt and pepper
¼	cup (50 mL) grated parmesan cheese

Wash and pierce squash deeply with knife in several places. Place in microwaveable pie plate. Microwave on High for 15 minutes or until squash yields to pressure, turning squash over after 7 minutes. Remove from microwave and let stand for 5 minutes. Cut in half and scrape out seeds and fibres; discard. Pull out long strands of flesh by twisting with a fork; put in large bowl.

While squash is cooking, stack spinach leaves and cut crosswise into thin strips; set aside.

In large heavy frypan, heat butter and oil over medium heat. Add onion and garlic; saute for 1 minute. Add spinach and saute for 2 to 3 minutes or until spinach is wilted. Transfer spinach mixture to small bowl.

Add ground lamb to same frypan and saute for 3 minutes or until cooked. Add spinach mixture, feta cheese and oregano; cook for 1 minute or until heated through. Add salt and pepper to taste. Add to squash and toss to coat.

Transfer to serving platter and sprinkle with parmesan cheese. ☡

TIP: Although both spaghetti squash and spaghetti pasta are low in fat, a 1-cup (250 mL) serving of cooked spaghetti squash has 46 calories, 1 gram protein, 0.4 grams fat and 10.2 grams carbohydrate; while a cup of cooked spaghetti pasta has 200 calories, 6.8 grams protein, 1 gram fat and 40.2 grams carbohydrate.

Bottom line: An equal amount of cooked spaghetti squash has far fewer calories than cooked spaghetti pasta.

Per serving:

408 calories, 20.8 g protein, 30.7 g fat, 13.9 g carbohydrate. Excellent source of vitamins A, B12, riboflavin, niacin and folate. Excellent source of calcium, iron, zinc, magnesium and phosphorus.

Lamb Chops with Lemon, Rosemary and Thyme

Makes 4 servings

Lamb and rosemary are a time-honoured pairing; here, thyme adds dynamic intrigue to the mix. This simple preparation, with its herbs, lemon and garlic, can be cooked in mere minutes. Serve with small new potatoes and tender-crisp asparagus or sugar snap peas.

8	loin lamb chops, about 1-inch (2.5 cm) thick
2	tablespoons (30 mL) olive oil
1	teaspoon (5 mL) finely grated lemon zest
1	teaspoon (5 mL) lemon juice
2	large garlic cloves, minced
1½	teaspoons (7 mL) finely chopped fresh rosemary
1½	teaspoons (7 mL) finely chopped fresh thyme
	Salt and pepper

Trim excess fat from lamb chops. In small bowl, combine oil, lemon zest, lemon juice, garlic, rosemary, thyme, ¾ teaspoon (4 mL) salt and ¼ teaspoon (1 mL) pepper.

Place lamb chops on greased broiler pan and brush with half the oil mixture; broil for 4 minutes. Turn chops and brush with remaining oil mixture; broil for 4 minutes or until chops are cooked to desired doneness. Season to taste with salt and pepper. 🕐

Per serving:
247 calories, 27.1 g protein, 14.6 g fat, 0.1 g carbohydrate. Excellent source of vitamin B12 and niacin. Excellent source of zinc.

Lamb Chops with Lentils and Rosemary

Makes 4 servings

Earthy, homey lentils have an affinity for lamb — the two balance each other. In this dish, they're intertwined by notes of rosemary, sage and simmered vegetables. A fresh green salad topped with crisp paper-thin fennel slices and halved cherry tomatoes makes a fine accompaniment.

3	tablespoons (45 mL) **vegetable oil, divided**
1	**onion, chopped fine**
2	**garlic cloves, minced**
1	**carrot, diced fine**
1	**stalk celery, diced fine**
1	**tablespoon (15 mL) chopped fresh sage**
1	**tablespoon (15 mL) chopped fresh rosemary, divided**
1	**cup (250 mL) red lentils**
1¾	**cups (425 mL) chicken stock**
2	**tablespoons (30 mL) grainy mustard (with seeds)**
8	**loin lamb chops, about 1-inch (2.5 cm) thick**
	Salt and pepper
	Chopped fresh parsley

In large heavy frypan, heat 1 tablespoon (15 mL) oil over medium heat. Add onion, garlic, carrot, celery, sage and 2 teaspoons (10 mL) rosemary; saute for 6 minutes or until vegetables are tender-crisp.

Stir in lentils and stock. Cover and simmer for 10 to 12 minutes or until liquid is absorbed and lentils are tender.

Meanwhile, combine mustard, remaining 2 tablespoons (30 mL) oil and remaining 1 teaspoon (5 mL) rosemary; set aside.

Trim excess fat from lamb chops. Sprinkle chops with salt and pepper. Place chops on greased broiler pan and brush tops with half the mustard mixture. Broil for 8 minutes or until cooked to desired doneness, turning once and brushing with remaining mustard mixture.

Season lentils with ¼ teaspoon (1 mL) each salt and pepper; transfer to serving platter and top with lamb chops. Sprinkle with parsley. ♺

TIP: Unlike other dried legumes, there is no need to soak lentils in water. Red lentils cook very quickly; in fact they require less time than brown or green lentils, so watch that you don't overcook them — they can disintegrate quickly.

Per serving:
467 calories, 40.1 g protein, 18.7 g fat, 34.6 g carbohydrate. Excellent source of vitamins A, B6, B12, thiamin, riboflavin and niacin. Excellent source of iron, zinc, magnesium and phosphorus. High in fibre.

Easy Blender Spaghetti Sauce

Makes 4 servings

TIP: Don't try to substitute cooking onion for the shallot; we did, and the result was a sauce with a sharp, harsh flavour.

Oh no, where's the Classico? Don't despair, just look a little deeper into your kitchen cupboard and dinner can still be on the table in half an hour. The trick to week-in-week-out fast cooking is to keep that cupboard well stocked with emergency items. Two good examples: 398 mL cans of tomatoes and 213 mL cans of tomato sauce. Together they do the job when the last jar of pasta sauce has vanished.

Why bother to make pasta sauce from scratch? For starters, it can be cheaper than store-bought. Even better, this one has a smooth, light taste. Put your blender to work while the ground beef is sauteing, then pour the tomato mixture over the meat and simmer. Meanwhile, you can boil the spaghetti and prepare a tossed green salad.

1	tablespoon (15 mL) vegetable oil
½	pound (250 g) lean ground beef
1	(398 mL) can tomatoes
1	shallot, chopped coarse
2	garlic cloves, smashed
1	teaspoon (5 mL) granulated sugar
1	teaspoon (5 mL) dried oregano leaves
½	teaspoon (2 mL) salt
¼	teaspoon (1 mL) pepper
	Hot pepper sauce
1	(213 mL) can tomato sauce
¾	pound (350 g) spaghetti
¼	cup (50 mL) grated parmesan cheese

In 12-inch (30 cm) heavy frypan, heat oil over medium-high heat. Add ground beef and saute for 3 minutes or until browned.

In blender, combine tomatoes, shallot, garlic, sugar, oregano, salt, pepper and hot pepper sauce to taste; blend at high speed for 60 seconds. Add tomato sauce and blend for 10 seconds.

Pour tomato mixture over beef in frypan; bring to a boil, reduce heat and simmer for 18 minutes or until sauce is slightly thickened, stirring occasionally.

Meanwhile, cook spaghetti in large pot of boiling salted water until tender; drain.

Serve tomato sauce over pasta. Sprinkle with parmesan cheese. ♻

Per serving:
601 calories, 26.8 g protein, 18.4 g fat, 81.3 g carbohydrate. Excellent source of vitamins B6, B12 and niacin. Excellent source of iron, zinc, magnesium and phosphorus.

Fusilli with Italian Sausage and Rapini

Makes 4 servings

For a fast, satisfying dinner with a taste of Italy, you can't go wrong with pasta as a base, then add the gusto of rapini and well-spiced sausages. Rapini, a hearty green, has an assertive, slightly bitter flavour when eaten on its own, but it blends well when balanced by other ingredients. It can usually be found in Italian produce markets as well as other places serving a Mediterranean clientele. Add a loaf of hearty bread — perhaps one studded with green or black olives, to extend the Mediterranean theme — and dinner's done.

4	cups (1 L) fusilli
¾	pound (350 g) hot Italian sausages, casings removed
1	tablespoon (15 mL) olive oil
1	pound (500 g) rapini, trimmed and cut into 1-inch (2.5 cm) pieces (about 8 cups/2 L)
1	red bell pepper, sliced thin
2	garlic cloves, minced
1	cup (250 mL) chicken stock
⅓	cup (75 mL) golden raisins
1	tablespoon (15 mL) butter
¼	cup (50 mL) chopped fresh parsley
	Salt and pepper
¼	cup (50 mL) grated parmesan cheese

Cook fusilli in large pot of boiling salted water until tender; drain and return to pot.

Meanwhile, cook sausage in large heavy frypan over medium heat for 5 minutes or until cooked, stirring and breaking up any lumps. With slotted spoon, transfer sausage to plate and set aside.

Add oil to frypan and increase heat to medium-high. Add rapini and red pepper; saute for 3 minutes. Add garlic, stock and raisins; simmer for 2 minutes or until rapini is tender, stirring and scraping browned bits from bottom of pan. Return sausage to frypan; stir in butter and cook for 1 minute or until heated through.

Add sausage mixture to pasta and toss. Stir in parsley, and salt and pepper to taste. Transfer to serving platter. Sprinkle with parmesan cheese. ☾

TIP: Rapini, also called rabe, broccoli raab and brocoletti di rape, looks like a skinny version of broccoli with its slender stalks and small broccoli-like florets. Stronger tasting than broccoli, its marries well with pasta, eggs and polenta. Cook quickly — rapini will lose its bright green colour if overcooked.

Per serving:
785 calories, 29.2 g protein, 37.2 g fat, 83.5 g carbohydrate. Excellent source of vitamins A, B6, B12, C, thiamin, riboflavin, niacin and folate. Excellent source of iron, zinc, magnesium and phosphorus. High in fibre.

Penne with Bell Peppers, Goat Cheese and Basil

Makes 4 servings

Every harried cook needs a handful of fine, fast pasta dishes in his or her repertoire — ones that go together in a flash and are suave enough to serve should the boss arrive for dinner unexpectedly. This is one of those. Bold strokes of pancetta and olives play off hot pepper hits, and creamy goat cheese brings it all together. Our first pasta choice is penne — little tubes, about the thickness of a pencil, often cut on the diagonal. They're hollow, which helps carry more sauce.

4	cups (1 L) penne
2	tablespoons (30 mL) olive oil
2	ounces (60 g) pancetta (Italian bacon), chopped
1	small onion, chopped fine
3	garlic cloves, minced
¼	teaspoon (1 mL) dried crushed hot red pepper
1	red bell pepper, sliced thin
1	yellow bell pepper, sliced thin
½	cup (125 mL) chicken stock
⅓	cup (75 mL) nicoise olives, pitted and halved
½	cup (125 mL) shredded fresh basil, divided
¼	teaspoon (1 mL) salt
¼	teaspoon (1 mL) pepper
½	cup (125 mL) plus 3 tablespoons (45 mL) unripened soft goat cheese (about 6 ounces/170 g total)

Cook penne in large pot of boiling salted water until tender; drain and return to pot, reserving ⅔ cup (150 mL) pasta water.

Meanwhile, heat oil in large heavy frypan over medium heat. Add pancetta and saute for 2 to 3 minutes or until crisp. Using slotted spoon, transfer pancetta to paper-towel-lined plate.

Increase heat to medium-high. Add onion, garlic and dried red pepper; saute for 3 minutes or until onion is tender. Add red and yellow bell peppers; saute for 2 minutes or until just tender. Add stock and olives; cook for 2 minutes or until reduced by half. Add ¼ cup (50 mL) basil, salt and pepper; remove from heat.

In bowl, whisk ½ cup (125 mL) goat cheese with reserved ⅔ cup (150 mL) pasta water until cheese mixture is smooth.

Add vegetables and cheese mixture to pasta; toss. Transfer to serving platter. Sprinkle with 3 tablespoons (45 mL) goat cheese (cut in small pieces), pancetta and remaining basil. ⟳

GREAT FOR ENTERTAINING

Per serving:
582 calories, 21.8 g protein, 21.1 g fat, 76.9 g carbohydrate. Excellent source of vitamins A, C, niacin and folate. Excellent source of iron and magnesium. High in fibre.

Rotini with Broccoli, Tomato and Prosciutto

Makes 4 servings

If carrots and broccoli aren't high on your children's list of favourites, then sneak them in with foods they do like — pasta, for example. The vegetables in this dish combine with prosciutto, sun-dried tomatoes and parmesan cheese, all the better to entice. If the youngsters already like carrots and broccoli, make this a frequent supper dish.

3	cups (750 mL) rotini
1	cup (250 mL) purchased, ready-to-use peeled mini carrots
3	cups (750 mL) small broccoli florets
2	tablespoons (30 mL) vegetable oil
1	onion, halved lengthwise and sliced thin
1	large garlic clove, minced
1	small red bell pepper, cut into thin strips
¼	pound (125 g) prosciutto (Italian ham), chopped
¼	cup (50 mL) slivered, drained sun-dried tomatoes (packed in oil)
	Pinch dried crushed hot red pepper
2	tablespoons (30 mL) water
2	tablespoons (30 mL) chopped fresh basil
¼	cup (50 mL) chopped fresh parsley
⅓	cup (75 mL) grated parmesan cheese
	Salt and pepper

Cook rotini in large pot of boiling salted water until tender, adding carrots 7 minutes before end of pasta cooking time and adding broccoli for the last 2 minutes. Drain pasta, broccoli and carrots; return to pot.

Meanwhile, heat oil in large heavy frypan over medium-high heat. Add onion, garlic and red bell pepper; saute for 3 minutes or until onion is tender. Add prosciutto, sun-dried tomatoes and dried red pepper; saute for 1 to 2 minutes or until heated through. Add water, stirring and scraping browned bits from bottom of pan. Add to pasta mixture along with basil, parsley, parmesan cheese, and salt and pepper to taste. Transfer to serving platter. ⟳

WHAT IS PROSCIUTTO?

Italy's most famous ham, prosciutto di Parma, is the one by which all others are judged. But similar hams are now produced in many places, including Canada. Prosciutto is a broad term for ham that is seasoned, salt-cured (but not smoked) and air-dried. Its unique firm, dense texture is the result of the meat having been pressed. It is usually sold in almost transparently thin slices.

Prosciutto can be pricey, but a little goes a long way, and nothing else gives dishes quite the same flavour boost.

TIME SAVER: Purchase washed, ready-to-use broccoli and mini carrots: A 340 gram package yields 3 cups (750 mL) broccoli and 1 cup (250 mL) mini carrots.

Per serving:
464 calories, 20.8 g protein, 13.2 g fat, 65.7 g carbohydrate. Excellent source of vitamins A, C, thiamin and niacin. Excellent source of magnesium. High in fibre.

Mediterranean Salad Pizza
Makes 4 to 6 servings

SUBSTITUTION: If you prefer, mesclun (a mix of young salad greens) could be substituted for the arugula. Mesclun can be found in ready-to-use packages in the produce section of supermarkets.

Is it a salad or a pizza? It's both. And it was love at first bite when our taste panel tried it. Unadorned flavours of sunny climes shine in this delicious pizza. As always, when the presentation is simple, the ingredients should be the best quality you can afford. One pleasantly unusual aspect of this pizza is the topping of fresh arugula — it adds some crunch and a distinctive peppery bite. If you'd like a meatless version, simply omit the prosciutto. Serve slices of canary melon or cantaloupe with a splash of lime juice for a quick, easy dessert.

2½	cups (625 mL) grated mozzarella cheese
2	(12-inch/30 cm) purchased, prebaked thin pizza crusts
1	cup (250 mL) thinly sliced sweet onion
4	plum tomatoes, sliced thin
2	garlic cloves, minced
½	cup (125 mL) pitted kalamata olives, halved
¼	pound (125 g) thinly sliced prosciutto (Italian ham), cut into large pieces
½	cup (125 mL) shaved parmesan cheese (about 2 ounces/60 g)
4	cups (1 L) torn arugula leaves
4	teaspoons (20 mL) extra-virgin olive oil
	Coarsely ground pepper

For each pizza: Sprinkle half the mozzarella cheese evenly over pizza crust. Arrange half the onion and tomatoes on top. Sprinkle with half the garlic. Bake at 450 F (230 C) for 10 minutes or until cheese is melted and toppings are hot.

Remove pizza from oven and top with half the olives and prosciutto. Top with half the parmesan cheese, then half the arugula. Drizzle with half the oil. Sprinkle with pepper to taste. ☾

Per serving:
997 calories, 44.6 g protein, 34.2 g fat, 126 g carbohydrate. Excellent source of vitamin B12, thiamin, riboflavin, niacin and folate. Excellent source of calcium, iron, zinc and phosphorus. Very high in fibre.

Goat Cheese and Cherry Tomato Pizza

Makes 4 to 6 servings

The red of the tomatoes, the green of the basil and near-white mozzarella combine to echo the colours of the Italian flag, and with the other intense ingredients (dark olives, prosciutto), the combination of flavours does, too. Depending on how quickly you slice and chop the toppings, this pizza can easily be ready to eat in 15 minutes. While the pizza bakes, slice some fresh fruit — strawberries, perhaps, or mangoes — if you'd like to end with a refreshing dessert.

2	(12-inch/30 cm) purchased, prebaked thin pizza crusts
1½	cups (375 mL) grated mozzarella cheese
½	cup (125 mL) chopped, drained sun-dried tomatoes (packed in oil)
½	cup (125 mL) pitted kalamata olives, chopped coarse
½	small red onion, sliced thin
2	cups (500 mL) cherry tomatoes, halved
2	tablespoons (30 mL) chopped fresh thyme
¼	cup (50 mL) unripened soft goat cheese, cut into small pieces
2	ounces (60 g) prosciutto (Italian ham), chopped Pepper
½	cup (125 mL) chopped fresh basil

For each pizza: Sprinkle pizza crust with half the mozzarella cheese. Top with half the sun-dried tomatoes, olives and onion. Arrange half the cherry tomatoes (cut side up) evenly over top, then sprinkle with half the thyme, goat cheese and prosciutto.

Bake at 450 F (230 C) for 10 minutes or until cheese is melted and toppings are hot. Lightly sprinkle with pepper and half the basil. ○

TIP: Although we don't think there is anything that delivers flavour quite like that of prosciutto (Italian ham), you could substitute another sliced ham; try Black Forest.

Per serving:

770 calories, 28.9 g protein, 23 g fat, 111 g carbohydrate. Excellent source of thiamin, riboflavin, niacin and folate. Excellent source of calcium, iron, zinc and phosphorus. High in fibre.

Caramelized Onion and Prosciutto Pizza

Makes 4 to 6 servings

The next time you face spur-of-the-moment entertaining, treat your guests (and yourself) to pizza rich in flavour. When you pair caramelized onions with three fine cheeses — presto! You get a fine, fast topping. Prosciutto, the luxuriously silky Italian ham, provides the meat element (increase the amount if you have a highly carnivorous crowd, or drop it entirely for a vegetarian version). The pizza needs nothing more to accompany it than a crisp tossed salad, which can be prepared once the pizza is in the oven.

1	tablespoon (15 mL) butter
1	tablespoon (15 mL) vegetable oil
2	large sweet onions (about 1 pound/500 g total), sliced
¼	teaspoon (1 mL) brown sugar
1	tablespoon (15 mL) balsamic vinegar
	Salt and pepper
2	cups (500 mL) grated mozzarella cheese
1	cup (250 mL) grated smoked gouda cheese
2	(12-inch/30 cm) purchased, prebaked thin pizza crusts
2	ounces (60 g) prosciutto (Italian ham), chopped coarse
¼	cup (50 mL) grated parmesan cheese
¼	cup (50 mL) shredded fresh basil

In 12-inch (30 cm) heavy frypan, heat butter and oil over medium heat. Add onions and saute for 15 minutes or until very tender, stirring occasionally. Sprinkle with brown sugar and vinegar; stir for 1 minute. Remove from heat, and add salt and pepper to taste.

Meanwhile, combine mozzarella and gouda cheeses. **For each pizza**: Sprinkle ¾ cup (175 mL) cheese mixture evenly over pizza crust. Top with half the onion mixture. Sprinkle with half the prosciutto and ¾ cup (175 mL) cheese mixture. Sprinkle with half the parmesan cheese.

Bake at 450 F (230 C) for 10 minutes or until cheese is melted and toppings are hot. Sprinkle with half the basil.

Triple-Duty Black Bean Chili

Makes 8 servings (about 9 cups/2.25 L)

This black bean chili recipe is the embodiment of flexibility, and it makes the most of your time in the kitchen. Prepare one batch using this full recipe, and you can serve half right away, simply as regular chili, with crusty rolls or cornbread. Or make it the base of the Warm Taco Salad (page 56). The other half of what you prepare is a bonus: Turn it into burritos (page 55), to be individually wrapped and frozen, ready for the family to thaw and reheat as needed. Another option is to freeze the chili as is — ready to reheat and serve in bowls or use in the taco salad.

1	tablespoon (15 mL) vegetable oil
1	pound (500 g) lean ground beef
2	onions, chopped
3	garlic cloves, minced
½	cup (125 mL) chopped celery
½	cup (125 mL) chopped red bell pepper
1	(796 mL) can tomatoes (undrained), chopped
1	(398 mL) can tomato sauce
5	teaspoons (25 mL) chili powder
1	bay leaf
½	teaspoon (2 mL) dried basil leaves
½	teaspoon (2 mL) dried oregano leaves
½	teaspoon (2 mL) hot chipotle pepper sauce
	Pinch granulated sugar
2	(398 mL) cans black beans, drained and rinsed
	Salt and pepper

In large heavy pot, heat oil over medium-high heat. Add ground beef, onions, garlic, celery and red pepper; saute for 5 minutes or until beef is brown and vegetables are tender, breaking beef up well and stirring frequently. Drain off juices and discard.

Add tomatoes, tomato sauce, chili powder, bay leaf, basil, oregano, chipotle pepper sauce and sugar; bring to a boil over medium-high heat. Reduce heat to low and simmer, covered, for 15 minutes, stirring occasionally.

Stir in beans and increase heat to medium-low; cook, uncovered, for 5 minutes or until heated through and slightly thickened. Remove bay leaf and discard. Add salt and pepper to taste. ⏲

FREEZING CHILI

Divide cooled chili in half; put each portion into a 5-cup (1.25 L) freezer container. For convenience, use round plastic freezer containers that are smaller than the saucepan or bowl you plan to reheat it in. Store in freezer for up to 1 month. If possible, partially thaw chili in refrigerator overnight to shorten reheating time.

REHEATING CHILI

Microwave oven: Run warm water over plastic freezer container to loosen chili. Remove chili to microwaveable bowl and cover with plastic wrap, turning back one corner to allow steam to escape. Microwave on High for 15 to 18 minutes, stirring every 2 minutes.

Stove-top: Run warm water over plastic freezer container to loosen chili. Remove chili to large heavy saucepan; add ¼ cup (50 mL) water. Cook, covered, over medium heat for 35 minutes or until hot, stirring frequently.

Per serving:
269 calories, 19 g protein, 11.3 g fat, 24.4 g carbohydrate. Excellent source of vitamin B12, niacin and folate. Excellent source of iron, zinc and magnesium. Very high in fibre.

Frozen Asset Chili Burritos

Makes 8 burritos

This is a perfect solution for busy families that find themselves eating in shifts. Our Triple-Duty Black Bean Chili is the basis for the burrito filling. Freeze the burritos in individual packages, ready to pop in the microwave for a quick snack or meal.

Burritos

4	**cups (1 L) Triple-Duty Black Bean Chili (page 54), cooled**
8	**(10-inch/25 cm) flour tortillas**

Toppings

8	**tablespoons (120 mL) finely grated cheddar cheese**
	Light sour cream, optional
	Mild or medium salsa, optional

Burritos: For each of 8 burritos, spoon about ½ cup (125 mL) chili in a mound across the bottom half of tortilla (side closest to you). Bring bottom edge of tortilla (side closest to you) up over filling and roll up to enclose filling. Wrap completely in plastic wrap; place wrapped burritos in single layer in large plastic freezer bag. Freeze for up to 1 month. ⟳

Note of caution: For food safety, if you're going to freeze these burritos, use only freshly made chili, not previously frozen.

REHEATING FROZEN BURRITOS

Microwave oven: Unwrap 1 frozen burrito and place seam side down on plate. Microwave on High for 1 minute. Sprinkle 1 tablespoon (15 mL) cheddar cheese over top. Microwave for 1 minute longer or until heated through. Serve with sour cream and salsa.

Conventional oven: Unwrap frozen burritos and place seam side down, in single layer, on rimmed baking sheet (with space between them). Bake at 350 F (180 C) for 30 minutes or until heated through, sprinkling each burrito with 1 tablespoon (15 mL) cheese about 5 minutes before end of reheating time. Serve with sour cream and salsa.

Per burrito (without sour cream or salsa):

280 calories, 14.3 g protein, 11.1 g fat, 32.3 g carbohydrate. Excellent source of vitamin B12, thiamin and folate. Excellent source of zinc. High in fibre.

Warm Taco Salad

Makes 4 servings

With extra portions of our Triple-Duty Black Bean Chili on hand (either freshly made or in the freezer), this bold, warm salad is a snap to make. Part of the salad's charm is that it's a bit messy, so dive right in. Tortilla chips are handy for dipping into the chili. Fruit salad would provide a refreshing finale.

- 8 cups (2 L) shredded romaine or iceberg lettuce
- 4 cups (1 L) tortilla chips
- 4 cups (1 L) Triple-Duty Black Bean Chili (page 54), heated
- 1 cup (250 mL) chopped tomato
- 1 cup (250 mL) finely grated cheddar cheese
- 4 tablespoons (60 mL) light sour cream
- Chopped green onion or fresh cilantro, optional

For each serving: Place 2 cups (500 mL) lettuce in large shallow soup bowl or on plate. Arrange 1 cup (250 mL) tortilla chips around edge of bowl. Spoon 1 cup (250 mL) hot chili on top of lettuce. Top with ¼ cup (50 mL) chopped tomato, ¼ cup (50 mL) cheddar cheese and 1 tablespoon (15 mL) sour cream. Sprinkle with chopped green onion. ⏲

TIP: Corn tortilla chips now come in an array of colours and flavours beyond the traditional yellow chip — select from the wide variety and add dazzle to your warm taco salad (for example, blue corn chips, red chips made with natural vegetable colour, chipotle-flavoured chips with their smoky spiciness).

TIME SAVER: Purchase washed, ready-to-use torn romaine lettuce: A 283 gram package yields about 10 cups (2.5 L).

Per serving:
634 calories, 33.4 g protein, 31.3 g fat, 60 g carbohydrate. Excellent source of vitamins A, B6, B12, C, thiamin, riboflavin, niacin and folate. Excellent source of iron, zinc, magnesium and phosphorus. Very high in fibre.

CHAPTER TWO

POULTRY

If God grants me longer life,
I will see to it that no peasant in my
kingdom will lack the
means to have a chicken in the pot
every Sunday.

Henry IV of France

Chicken and Spinach Alphabet Soup

Makes 4 servings

There is no denying commercial canned soups are more convenient than home-made, but they will never compare to the rich, flavourful ones made in your own kitchen. Home-made soups need not take hours of preparation; this one can be on the table in about 30 minutes.

The health benefits of chicken soup were once considered an old wives' tale; now science is confirming what Mom knew well. So eat up. If the kids are ravenous, add a simple sandwich.

1	tablespoon (15 mL) olive oil
1	onion, chopped
2	large carrots, cut in half lengthwise and sliced thin
2	stalks celery, chopped
8	cups (2 L) chicken stock
⅓	cup (75 mL) alphabet pasta
½	pound (250 g) boneless skinless chicken thighs, cut into ½-inch (1 cm) pieces
2	cups (500 mL) shredded fresh spinach
½	teaspoon (2 mL) dried thyme leaves
	Salt and pepper

In large heavy saucepan, heat oil over medium-high heat. Add onion, carrots and celery; saute for 5 minutes. Add stock, cover and increase heat to high; bring to a boil. Add alphabet pasta and boil, partially covered, for 8 minutes.

Add chicken thighs, spinach and thyme to soup; reduce heat and simmer for 3 minutes or until chicken is cooked and pasta is tender. Add salt and pepper to taste. ○

TIME SAVERS

• Buy ready-to-use chicken broth found in cartons, and packaged washed, ready-to-use fresh spinach.

• You can easily double the payoff for time invested in home-made soup by doubling this recipe: Serve some for supper and stash the rest away in the freezer for another weekday meal.

SUBSTITUTION: Any other small pasta could be used — try little shells, small bows or orzo (rice-shaped pasta).

Per serving:

176 calories, 15.2 g protein, 6.3 g fat, 15.1 g carbohydrate. Excellent source of vitamin A and niacin.

Turkey Tortilla Soup
Makes 5 servings

TIP: We prefer to use
unsalted corn tortilla chips —
if your favourite brand of
tortilla chips is salted, then
adjust the amount of salt you
add accordingly.

*Just a spoonful or two of this heart-warming midweek soup will have
you dreaming of a warm Mexican beach. It's spicy, robust and, yes, we
added those tortilla chips — they didn't just fall in. Heat-loving chili-
heads will want to increase the hot pepper sauce to taste.*

1	tablespoon (15 mL) olive oil
1	onion, chopped
2	garlic cloves, minced
1	teaspoon (5 mL) chili powder
7	cups (1.75 L) chicken stock
1	(398 mL) can stewed tomatoes
1	(398 mL) can red kidney or black beans, drained and rinsed
1	(199 mL) can whole kernel corn, drained
2	cups (500 mL) diced cooked turkey breast (about ½ pound/250 g)
1	cup (250 mL) coarsely broken, unsalted corn tortilla chips
¼	teaspoon (1 mL) chipotle or other hot pepper sauce
2	teaspoons (10 mL) lime juice
	Salt and pepper
¼	cup (50 mL) light sour cream
¼	cup (50 mL) chopped fresh cilantro

In large heavy saucepan, heat oil over medium-high heat.
Add onion and garlic; saute for 3 minutes. Add chili powder and
saute for 1 minute. Add stock, stewed tomatoes, beans, corn,
turkey, tortilla chips and hot pepper sauce; bring to a boil over high
heat, reduce heat and simmer for 1 minute. Stir in lime juice, and
salt and pepper to taste.

To serve, top with a dollop of sour cream and sprinkle with
cilantro. ⊘

Per serving:

282 calories, 22.7 g protein, 7.2 g fat,
33.6 g carbohydrate. Excellent source
of niacin and folate. Excellent source
of magnesium. Very high in fibre.

Spinach Salad with Turkey and Strawberries

Makes 6 servings

A Fraser Valley Strawberry Growers' Association recipe was the inspiration for this light salad. Sweet strawberries and fresh baby spinach are enhanced with a tangy balsamic vinaigrette. This simple salad is elevated by the addition of sugared almonds, contributing to a good balance of flavour, texture and colour.

Sugared almonds

½	cup (125 mL) slivered almonds
¼	cup (50 mL) granulated sugar
1	tablespoon (15 mL) water

Dressing

4	teaspoons (20 mL) balsamic vinegar
2	teaspoons (10 mL) worcestershire sauce
2	teaspoons (10 mL) liquid honey
1¼	teaspoons (6 mL) poppy seeds
2	teaspoons (10 mL) finely chopped fresh chives
3	tablespoons (45 mL) olive oil
	Salt and pepper

Salad

8	cups (2 L) lightly packed fresh baby spinach
½	pound (250 g) cold roast turkey, shredded into small pieces
2	cups (500 mL) sliced strawberries

Sugared almonds: In medium-size heavy saucepan, combine almonds, sugar and water. Cook over medium-low heat for 5 to 10 minutes or until sugar is almost completely melted and nuts are golden, stirring constantly (there will be a few grains of unmelted sugar on nuts). Spread nuts on pan; let cool and break into small pieces. *(Make-ahead: Nuts can be stored in air-tight container for up to 3 days.)*

Dressing: In small bowl, whisk together vinegar, worcestershire sauce, honey, poppy seeds and chives; whisk in oil. Add salt and pepper to taste.

Salad: In large bowl, toss spinach with turkey and strawberries. Add dressing and toss gently until lightly coated. Add nuts, toss lightly and serve. ⟳

TIME SAVERS

- Purchase washed, ready-to-use fresh baby spinach: A 170 gram package yields about 8 cups (2 L) lightly packed.

- Substitute toasted slivered almonds for the sugared almonds. To toast slivered almonds, spread nuts on rimmed baking sheet and bake at 350 F (180 C) for 4 to 6 minutes or until fragrant and golden.

SUBSTITUTION: We bought roast turkey from the deli, but you could also grill 3 boneless skinless chicken breasts; slice thin and place an equal portion of hot chicken on top of each salad.

Per serving:

256 calories, 13.4 g protein, 15.7 g fat, 18.2 g carbohydrate. Excellent source of vitamins A, B12, C, niacin and folate. Excellent source of magnesium.

Some-Like-It-Hot Chicken Salad

Makes 4 servings

¼ cup (50 mL) white balsamic vinegar

¼ cup (50 mL) white wine vinegar

1 teaspoon (5 mL) dijon mustard

½ teaspoon (2 mL) liquid honey

1 teaspoon (5 mL) salt

½ teaspoon (2 mL) pepper

6 tablespoons (90 mL) olive oil

In small bowl, whisk together all ingredients. Makes about ¾ cup (175 mL). You'll only need 5 tablespoons (75 mL) for the chicken salad; refrigerate remaining vinaigrette for another use.

TIP: If you opt for a bottled vinaigrette, pick one with a tangy flavour. We used Maille's Provence Vinaigrette with olive oil, garlic and herbs.

Per serving:

263 calories, 33.4 g protein, 10.5 g fat, 8.1 g carbohydrate. Excellent source of vitamins A, B6, B12, C, niacin and folate. Excellent source of phosphorus.

Sturdy greens are the best choice for warm salads because they withstand some heat. Here we used one 283 gram package of washed, ready-to-use European salad blend (iceberg, romaine and green leaf lettuce, plus radicchio and endive). Add a few tender baby greens, if desired.

4 small boneless skinless chicken breasts, cut into thin strips (about 1 pound/500 g total)
  Salt and pepper

5 tablespoons (75 mL) vinaigrette, divided (purchased or home-made)

2 tablespoons (30 mL) vegetable oil, divided

2 ounces (60 g) thinly sliced prosciutto (Italian ham), chopped coarse

1 small onion, chopped

1 large garlic clove, minced

1 red bell pepper, cut into thin strips

8 cups (2 L) torn mixed sturdy salad greens

Lightly sprinkle chicken breast strips with salt and pepper; put in small bowl. Add 2 tablespoons (30 mL) vinaigrette; stir and let stand for 10 minutes.

Meanwhile, heat 1 tablespoon (15 mL) oil in large heavy frypan over medium-high heat. Add prosciutto and saute for 1 minute or until crisp. With slotted spoon, transfer prosciutto to small bowl and set aside. Add chicken to frypan and saute for 3 minutes or until no longer pink inside. With slotted spoon, transfer chicken to plate and keep warm. Discard any pan juices.

Add remaining 1 tablespoon (15 mL) oil to frypan. Add onion and garlic; saute for 2 minutes. Add red pepper and saute for 2 minutes or until tender-crisp. Return chicken to pan and heat through.

Add remaining 3 tablespoons (45 mL) vinaigrette to salad greens and toss. Add salt and pepper to taste. Arrange greens on large serving platter and top with hot chicken mixture and prosciutto. ◷

Mango Tango Grilled Chicken

Makes 4 servings

When mangoes come into season, just about the time we dust off the barbecue, it's the cue for a love affair with salsas. They can elevate an ordinary poultry, fish or meat dish into something sensational, and without much effort. This chicken is first flavoured with a balsamic marinade, then served with a fresh salsa that gets extra punch from lime juice, jalapeno pepper and cilantro. Serve with nugget potatoes, sprinkled with chopped parsley, plus steamed broccoli or swiss chard.

Grilled chicken

- **4 boneless skinless chicken breasts**
- **2 tablespoons (30 mL) balsamic vinegar**
- **1 tablespoon (15 mL) olive oil**
- **Pinch brown sugar**

Mango salsa

- **1 mango, peeled, pitted and chopped**
- **¼ cup (50 mL) diced English cucumber**
- **¼ cup (50 mL) chopped red onion**
- **2 tablespoons (30 mL) chopped fresh cilantro**
- **1 small jalapeno pepper, seeded and chopped fine**
- **2 tablespoons (30 mL) lime juice**
- **Salt and pepper**

Grilled chicken: Pound chicken breasts until ½-inch (1 cm) thick; place in shallow dish. In small bowl, whisk together vinegar, oil and brown sugar. Pour over chicken and turn to coat; let stand for 10 minutes.

Meanwhile, prepare salsa: In small bowl, combine mango, cucumber, onion, cilantro, jalapeno pepper and lime juice. Add salt and pepper to taste.

Place chicken on greased barbecue grill over medium-high heat and cook for 8 minutes or until no longer pink inside, turning once. Season with salt and pepper to taste. Serve with salsa.

WHERE'S THE HEAT?

Most of the heat is contained in the seeds and veins of hot peppers. Recipes often call for the seeds to be removed. This is easily done by slicing the pepper in half lengthwise using a paring knife, and with the tip of the knife, scraping out the seeds.

PEPPER STORAGE

Put jalapeno peppers in small paper bag and store in the refrigerator for up to 2 weeks.

SUBSTITUTION: Use 2 large peaches or nectarines instead of the mango.

Per serving:

210 calories, 29.5 g protein, 5.2 g fat, 10.9 g carbohydrate. Excellent source of vitamin B6 and niacin.

Grilled Chicken with Corn and Sun-Dried Tomato Salsa

Makes 4 servings

Dried tomatoes deliver an intense punch that's far different from the flavour of a ripe fresh tomato. Take advantage of this powerful ingredient when you're a cook in a hurry. Here, sun-dried tomatoes pair well with a traditional partner, fresh corn, in a zesty salsa to accent chicken. A simple accompaniment can be red and yellow bell peppers (cut in quarters), cooked along side the chicken on the grill, then splashed with a little balsamic vinegar just before serving. Serve with texmati rice.

4	boneless skinless chicken breasts
4	tablespoons (60 mL) vegetable oil, divided
4	tablespoons (60 mL) lime juice, divided
1	teaspoon (5 mL) ground cumin
	Salt and pepper
2	large ears corn, kernels removed (about 1¾ cups/425 mL)
¼	cup (50 mL) finely chopped, drained sun-dried tomatoes (packed in oil)
¼	cup (50 mL) thinly sliced green onions
¼	cup (50 mL) finely chopped red onion
3	garlic cloves, minced
1	small jalapeno pepper, seeded and chopped fine
¼	cup (50 mL) chopped fresh cilantro

Place chicken breasts in shallow baking dish. In small bowl, combine 3 tablespoons (45 mL) oil, 2 tablespoons (30 mL) lime juice, cumin, and ¼ teaspoon (1 mL) each salt and pepper; pour over chicken, turning pieces to coat well. Let stand while preparing salsa.

Cook corn kernels in boiling water for 2 minutes or until tender-crisp; rinse with cold water and drain.

In bowl, stir together sun-dried tomatoes, green onions, red onion, garlic, jalapeno pepper, cilantro, remaining 2 tablespoons (30 mL) lime juice, remaining 1 tablespoon (15 mL) oil, ¼ teaspoon (1 mL) each salt and pepper, and cooked corn; set salsa aside.

Remove chicken from lime juice mixture and place on greased barbecue grill over medium-high heat. Cook for 10 to 12 minutes or until no longer pink inside, turning once.

Slice chicken thin and serve with salsa. ⟲

TIME SAVER: When fresh corn is not in season, or if you would like to reduce the preparation time, substitute 1 (341 mL) can whole kernel corn (drain well) for 2 large ears corn.

Per serving:

300 calories, 31.2 g protein, 10.4 g fat, 22.9 g carbohydrate. Excellent source of vitamin B6, niacin and folate. Excellent source of magnesium and phosphorus. High in fibre.

Speedy Lemon Chicken

Makes 4 servings

Quick, simple and oh so tasty — lemon chicken makes a perfect midweek dinner for family or friends. Here's the game plan: Put a pot of rice on to cook, then turn your attention to pounding and seasoning the chicken. This goes well with simply steamed or sauteed vegetables: asparagus, sliced zucchini, red bell pepper or Japanese eggplant — just one or a combination.

4	**boneless skinless chicken breasts**
2	**tablespoons (30 mL) lemon juice**
⅓	**cup (75 mL) all-purpose flour**
	Salt and pepper
1	**tablespoon (15 mL) butter**
1	**tablespoon (15 mL) vegetable oil**
	Chopped fresh parsley
4	**lemon wedges**

Pound chicken breasts until ¼-inch (5 mm) thick. Drizzle both sides with lemon juice.

On plate, combine flour, ½ teaspoon (2 mL) salt and ⅛ teaspoon (0.5 mL) pepper. Coat chicken with flour mixture, shaking off excess.

In large heavy frypan, heat butter and oil over medium-high heat. Add chicken and saute for 4 to 6 minutes or until no longer pink inside, turning once. Transfer to serving platter. Season to taste with salt and pepper. Sprinkle with parsley. Serve with lemon wedges.

TIP: Both heat and pressure make it easier to juice a lemon. Pierce whole lemon with a sharp knife and microwave on High for about 20 seconds, then roll under palm of hand on countertop until it softens slightly.

Per serving:

227 calories, 28.5 g protein, 8 g fat, 9.7 g carbohydrate. Excellent source of vitamin B6 and niacin.

Chicken Breasts with Fresh Herbs and Asiago

Makes 4 servings

Chicken breasts always come in handy if you're pressed for time — and who isn't? — and if you give them a good pounding first, they cook that much faster.

Rosemary, thyme, hot red pepper and asiago cheese mingle with bread crumbs to form a crisp, flavourful coating on these chicken breasts, locking moisture inside. Keep the rest of the meal simple and let this centrepiece shine. Saute an assortment of red, green and yellow bell pepper strips to serve along side the chicken and complete the course with basmati rice.

4	boneless skinless chicken breasts
⅓	cup (75 mL) all-purpose flour
½	teaspoon (2 mL) salt
½	teaspoon (2 mL) pepper
2	egg whites
1	cup (250 mL) fresh bread crumbs
⅓	cup (75 mL) grated asiago cheese
1	garlic clove, minced
1	tablespoon (15 mL) chopped fresh rosemary
1	tablespoon (15 mL) chopped fresh thyme
¼	teaspoon (1 mL) dried crushed hot red pepper

Pound chicken breasts until ¼-inch (5 mm) thick.

On plate, combine flour, salt and pepper. In bowl, lightly beat egg whites. In pie plate, combine bread crumbs, asiago cheese, garlic, rosemary, thyme and dried red pepper.

Coat chicken with flour mixture, shaking off excess. Dip in egg whites to coat completely, then coat with crumb mixture, shaking off excess. Place on greased baking sheet.

Bake at 400 F (200 C) for 15 minutes or until chicken is no longer pink inside. ⏱

TIPS

- Versatile and budget friendly — nothing beats boneless skinless chicken breasts for quick meal preparation. Another bonus: There's no waste — you get what you pay for. Boneless breasts with skin on are usually cheaper, but after factoring in the price of what you discard anyway, it's just as economical to buy boneless skinless breasts.

- To make fresh bread crumbs, tear up day-old bread slices and pop into a food processor. Pulse until coarse crumbs are formed.

Per serving:

329 calories, 36.4 g protein, 6.2 g fat, 29.1 g carbohydrate. Excellent source of vitamins B6, B12 and niacin. Excellent source of phosphorus.

Crispy Parmesan-Pecan Chicken

Makes 4 servings

Parmesan-coated chicken breasts are a classic, but classics lend themselves to subtle variations. Add pecans for something nutty and dijon mustard for a spicy edge, and the result is a keeper. The coating ensures the chicken stays moist and tender. Serve this with boiled small potatoes (we've seen bags of mixed red, purple and white spuds in produce stores), and green beans with a small knob of butter and chopped parsley.

When you get home, turn the oven on before you do anything else. Then, once you put the potatoes on to cook, you can turn your attention to the chicken. Once that's in the oven, then it's time to cook your green vegetable.

4	boneless skinless chicken breasts
	Salt and pepper
2	slices fresh white bread, torn into small pieces
½	cup (125 mL) grated parmesan cheese
¼	cup (50 mL) pecan halves
2	teaspoons (10 mL) melted butter
1	large egg, lightly beaten
4	teaspoons (20 mL) dijon mustard

Pound chicken breasts until ½-inch (1 cm) thick. Lightly sprinkle with salt and pepper.

In food processor, combine bread, parmesan cheese and pecans; pulse until nuts are finely chopped. Transfer to pie plate. Add butter, 1 teaspoon (5 mL) at a time, tossing with fork to mix.

In small bowl, whisk together egg and mustard. Dip chicken in egg mixture then in crumb mixture to coat evenly, shaking off excess. Place on greased baking sheet. Bake at 450 F (230 C) for 15 minutes or until chicken is no longer pink inside. ◔

TIPS

- Freshly grated parmesan cheese is a must for this crispy coating. Buy a chunk of parmesan and do the job yourself, or buy it freshly grated in the deli section of the supermarket. The dry, powdery parmesan sold in plastic containers from grocers' shelves can't compare to the taste and texture of good-quality Parmigiano-Reggiano, the real thing. Grana Padano is a reasonable second choice.

- Don't bake the chicken breasts on parchment-paper lined baking sheets — the coating will steam instead of becoming crisp and golden.

Per serving:

301 calories, 36 g protein, 12.8 g fat, 9 g carbohydrate. Excellent source of vitamins B6, B12 and niacin.

Brandied Sour-Cherry Chicken

Makes 4 servings

Break out the brandy for a fast, special-occasion dinner (even if it pains some members of the household to see brandy going into a saucepan). If they like brandy, they'll like this result, especially the combination of sour cherries, thyme, cream and liquor. A packaged pilaf mix and steamed broccoli take the work out of completing the meal.

1	cup (250 mL) chicken stock
¼	cup (50 mL) brandy
⅓	cup (75 mL) dried sour cherries
4	boneless skinless chicken breasts
	Salt and pepper
1	tablespoon (15 mL) butter
1	tablespoon (15 mL) vegetable oil
1	large shallot, chopped fine
1	teaspoon (5 mL) finely chopped fresh thyme
¼	teaspoon (1 mL) brown sugar
¼	cup (50 mL) whipping cream

In small saucepan, combine stock, brandy and cherries. Bring to a boil; reduce heat and simmer, covered, for 3 minutes or until cherries are plumped. Set aside.

Pound chicken breasts until ½-inch (1 cm) thick. Lightly sprinkle with salt and pepper.

In large heavy frypan, heat butter and oil over medium heat. Add chicken and saute for 8 minutes or until chicken is no longer pink inside, turning once. Transfer chicken to plate and keep warm.

Add shallot to frypan and saute for 30 seconds. Stir in cherry mixture and bring to a boil; cook for 3 minutes or until slightly thickened. Stir in thyme, brown sugar and cream; cook for 1 minute, stirring constantly. Add salt and pepper to taste. Transfer chicken to serving platter. Pour sauce over chicken. ⟳

SUBSTITUTION: Dried sour cherries, sometimes labelled by their variety, Montmorency, can be found in some public markets and bulk food stores. Dried sweet cherries are more common and can be substituted; if you use them, omit the brown sugar. You could also replace the cherries with dried cranberries, but don't omit the sugar.

Per serving:

270 calories, 28.1 g protein, 11.9 g fat, 8.5 g carbohydrate. Excellent source of vitamin B6 and niacin.

Mint and Ginger Chicken

Makes 4 servings

This fresh-tasting suave combination, with its hints of Indian and other Asian spicing, has long been a favourite with our tasters, making this fast recipe a winner. Basmati rice works well with this dish, especially if flavoured with chicken stock and flecked with sauteed chopped red bell pepper. While the chicken is lolling in the yogurt herb mixture, put the rice on to cook. Then, turn your attention to a colourful vegetable — sugar snap peas are perfect. Halved cherry or grape tomatoes drizzled with oil and vinegar and sprinkled with minced shallot would complement the main flavours.

1	cup (250 mL) plain yogurt
⅓	cup (75 mL) coarsely chopped fresh mint
¼	cup (50 mL) coarsely chopped fresh cilantro
¼	cup (50 mL) chopped green onions
1	tablespoon (15 mL) finely chopped fresh ginger
3	garlic cloves, crushed
¼	teaspoon (1 mL) ground cumin
1	tablespoon (15 mL) lemon juice
¼	teaspoon (1 mL) hot chili paste
4	boneless skinless chicken breasts
	Cilantro or mint sprigs

In bowl, combine yogurt, mint, chopped cilantro, green onions, ginger, garlic, cumin, lemon juice and chili paste; remove ¼ cup (50 mL) and set aside. Add chicken breasts to remaining yogurt mixture in bowl, turning to coat. Let marinate for 10 minutes.

Remove chicken from marinade (discarding any leftover marinade) and place on greased broiler pan; broil for 7 minutes. Turn over and brush chicken with reserved ¼ cup (50 mL) yogurt mixture; broil for another 7 minutes or until no longer pink inside (chicken will not brown). Garnish with cilantro sprigs. ♻

TIP: Select a bunch of fresh mint that shows no signs of wilting or discolouration. To prevent bruising, chop the mint with a very sharp chef's knife, or cut with scissors.

LOW | FAT

Per serving:

175 calories, 30.9 g protein, 2.5 g fat, 5.6 g carbohydrate. Excellent source of vitamins B6, B12 and niacin. Low in fat.

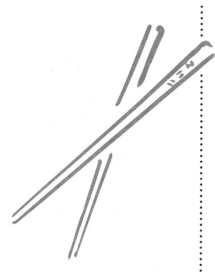

Nectarine and Ginger Chicken Stir-Fry

Makes 4 servings

There's sweet mirth in the interplay of nectarines, vegetables and spicy Asian flavours in this dish. It comes together quickly, so have the other elements of dinner set to go. Rice is the obvious starch option, so get that cooking before starting the chicken. Check well ahead that your pantry has the Asian ingredients called for: mirin, rice wine vinegar, soy sauce, hot chili paste.

2	tablespoons (30 mL) mirin (sweet Japanese rice wine) or dry sherry
1	tablespoon (15 mL) rice wine vinegar
1	tablespoon (15 mL) soy sauce
1	teaspoon (5 mL) hot chili paste or to taste
2	teaspoons (10 mL) cornstarch
2	tablespoons (30 mL) vegetable oil
1	tablespoon (15 mL) grated fresh ginger
2	garlic cloves, minced
4	small boneless skinless chicken breasts, cut into thin strips (about 1 pound/500 g total)
1	small red bell pepper, cut into ¼-inch (5 mm) strips
1	cup (250 mL) snow peas, trimmed and cut in half
2	large nectarines, cut into eighths
2	tablespoons (30 mL) chopped fresh cilantro
1	tablespoon (15 mL) chopped fresh mint

In small bowl, combine mirin, vinegar, soy sauce, hot chili paste and cornstarch; set aside.

In large wok or heavy frypan, heat oil over medium-high heat. Add ginger and garlic; stir-fry for 30 seconds. Add chicken and stir-fry for 2 minutes. Add red pepper, snow peas and nectarines; stir-fry for 2 minutes.

Whisk mirin mixture; add to wok and cook for 2 minutes or until sauce is slightly thickened, stirring constantly. Transfer to serving platter. Sprinkle with cilantro and mint. ↺

SUBSTITUTION: Vinegars vary in strength and flavour. Don't despair if you only have a couple of vinegars in your cupboard — you can substitute one kind for another in most recipes, but the amount you need might vary. When making a switch, start by adding half the amount called for in a recipe, taste, and then add more if necessary. A good stand-in for mild rice vinegar is a slightly reduced amount of cider vinegar: For every 1 tablespoon (15 mL) of rice vinegar, substitute 2 teaspoons (10 mL) apple cider vinegar and a pinch of granulated sugar.

Per serving:

267 calories, 29.5 g protein, 8.9 g fat, 15.4 g carbohydrate. Excellent source of vitamin C and niacin.

Curried Chicken Thighs with Chutney

Makes 4 servings

When you want chicken parts with flavour, go for thighs or drumsticks. Yes, they have more fat than milder chicken breasts, but when additional ingredients are kept in check, that's a minor concern. Lemon juice, mango chutney and a tease of curry paste give this dish flavour galore, so all the support it needs is plain basmati rice plus a simple salad and, if you can find them at your supermarket, some Indian flatbread: pappadams or naan.

1	pound (500 g) boneless skinless chicken thighs
	Salt and pepper
1	tablespoon (15 mL) butter
1	tablespoon (15 mL) vegetable oil
2	tablespoons (30 mL) finely chopped onion
1	large garlic clove, minced
⅓	cup (75 mL) chicken stock
1	tablespoon (15 mL) lemon juice
3	tablespoons (45 mL) mango chutney
1	teaspoon (5 mL) medium-hot Indian curry paste

Pound chicken thighs until ¼-inch (5 mm) thick. Cut each thigh in half crosswise. Lightly sprinkle with salt and pepper.

In large heavy frypan, heat butter and oil over medium-high heat. Add chicken and saute for 5 to 7 minutes or until cooked, turning once. Transfer chicken to plate and keep warm.

Drain off all but 1 tablespoon (15 mL) fat from frypan. Reduce heat to medium. Add onion and garlic to frypan; saute for 2 minutes or until onion is tender. Add stock, lemon juice, chutney and curry paste; boil for 2 to 3 minutes or until slightly thickened, stirring and scraping browned bits from bottom of pan. Add salt and pepper to taste. Transfer chicken to serving platter. Pour sauce over chicken. ⭕

TIP: Naan, a traditional flatbread of India, is now available in most supermarkets. Look for it near the prebaked pizza crusts in the bakery section. Heat bread according to package directions. If there are no instructions, use these times as a rough guide. Stack and wrap 4 breads in dampened tea towel and microwave on High for 30 to 45 seconds, or stack and wrap in foil and put in 425 F (220 C) oven for 5 to 8 minutes.

Per serving:

233 calories, 24.7 g protein, 11.3 g fat, 7.2 g carbohydrate. Excellent source of vitamin B6 and niacin.

Chicken Thighs with Port, Cranberries and Rosemary

Makes 4 servings

When old friends drop by for a quickly arranged dinner, keep this dish in mind. Chicken thighs aren't glamorous on their own, but given the royal treatment, they shine. If there isn't any port in the house, don't rush out and buy a bottle just for two tablespoons — substitute another fortified wine. Dried cranberries quickly add intense flavour — they're worth the price. Serve the chicken with orzo, tossed with a little olive oil and chopped basil, plus a green salad topped with goat cheese and croutons.

1   pound (500 g) boneless skinless chicken thighs
      Salt and pepper
1   tablespoon (15 mL) vegetable oil
1   shallot, chopped fine
¾   cup (175 mL) chicken stock
2   tablespoons (30 mL) port
1   tablespoon (15 mL) balsamic vinegar
⅓   cup (75 mL) dried cranberries
1   teaspoon (5 mL) finely chopped fresh rosemary

Pound chicken thighs until ¼-inch (5 mm) thick. Cut each thigh in half crosswise. Lightly sprinkle with salt and pepper.

In large heavy frypan, heat oil over medium-high heat. Add chicken and saute for 5 to 7 minutes or until cooked, turning once. Transfer chicken to plate and keep warm.

Reduce heat to medium and add shallot to frypan; saute for 30 seconds. Add stock, port, vinegar, cranberries and rosemary; boil for 3 to 4 minutes or until slightly thickened, stirring and scraping browned bits from bottom of pan. Add salt and pepper to taste. Transfer chicken to serving platter. Pour sauce over chicken. ⟳

Per serving:

206 calories, 26 g protein, 7.7 g fat, 4.8 g carbohydrate. Excellent source of niacin.

Chicken Thighs with Honey Mustard Sauce

Makes 4 servings

Sweet, alluring honey mustard almost qualifies as a ready-made sauce. Combined with stock, garlic and balsamic vinegar, it does wonders for chicken thighs. Add some mushrooms, and it could take on a grand-sounding French name, but why put on airs. This is simply good family fare, and the only sidekick it needs is a mixture of steamed seasonal vegetables and broad noodles tossed with a little butter.

1	pound (500 g) boneless skinless chicken thighs
	Salt and pepper
1	tablespoon (15 mL) vegetable oil
1	small onion, chopped
2	garlic cloves, minced
1	cup (250 mL) sliced mushrooms (3 ounces/85 g)
½	cup (125 mL) chicken stock
2	tablespoons (30 mL) balsamic vinegar
	Pinch brown sugar
¼	teaspoon (1 mL) dried basil leaves
1	teaspoon (5 mL) honey mustard

Pound chicken thighs until ¼-inch (5 mm) thick. Cut each thigh in half crosswise. Lightly sprinkle with salt and pepper.

In large heavy frypan, heat oil over medium-high heat. Add chicken and saute for 5 to 7 minutes or until cooked, turning once. Transfer chicken to plate and keep warm.

Add onion, garlic and mushrooms to frypan; saute for 2 to 3 minutes or until lightly browned. Add stock, vinegar, brown sugar and basil; boil for 2 minutes or until slightly thickened, stirring and scraping browned bits from bottom of pan. Stir in mustard. Add salt and pepper to taste. Transfer chicken to serving platter. Pour sauce over chicken. ○

TIP: Don't bother with an expensive balsamic vinegar for this recipe — the pinch of brown sugar and the little bit of cooking time will sweeten an everyday balsamic.

Per serving:

237 calories, 31.4 g protein, 9.6 g fat, 4.7 g carbohydrate. Excellent source of vitamins B6, B12 and niacin. Excellent source of phosphorus and zinc.

TIP: There are about 8 boneless skinless chicken thighs in 1 pound (500 g).

Chicken Thighs in Rosemary-Orange Sauce

Makes 4 servings

We know fanatics who would never dream of serving anything but their own home-made marmalade. That's great if you have the time to make it, but when you need an easy citrusy hit of flavour to make a sauce more complex, reach for a familiar store-bought jar. Mixed with sauteed onion, garlic, fresh orange juice, a bit of wine and fresh rosemary, any orange marmalade helps create a sauce with tang. Chicken takes well to sweetness, and that's the basis of this tempting combination. Serve with a crisp spinach salad, and pasta tossed with a little extra-virgin olive oil.

1	**pound (500 g) boneless skinless chicken thighs**
	Salt and pepper
1	**tablespoon (15 mL) butter**
1	**tablespoon (15 mL) vegetable oil**
¼	**cup (50 mL) finely chopped onion**
1	**garlic clove, minced**
½	**cup (125 mL) fresh orange juice**
¼	**cup (50 mL) orange marmalade**
1	**tablespoon (15 mL) dry white wine**
2	**teaspoons (10 mL) chopped fresh rosemary**

Pound chicken thighs until ¼-inch (5 mm) thick. Cut each thigh in half crosswise. Lightly sprinkle with salt and pepper.

In large heavy frypan, heat butter and oil over medium-high heat. Add chicken and saute for 5 to 7 minutes or until cooked, turning once. Transfer chicken to plate and keep warm.

Drain off all but 1 tablespoon (15 mL) fat from frypan. Add onion and garlic to frypan; saute for 2 minutes or until tender. Add orange juice, stirring and scraping browned bits from bottom of pan. Reduce heat to medium and stir in marmalade, wine and rosemary; cook for 2 to 3 minutes or until slightly thickened. Add salt and pepper to taste. Transfer chicken to serving platter. Pour sauce over chicken. ⏱

Per serving:

241 calories, 25 g protein, 7.9 g fat, 16 g carbohydrate. Excellent source of niacin.

Chicken Thighs with Curried Couscous

Makes 4 servings

Once anyone has cooked couscous, the tiniest of pasta grains, for a few meals, it becomes a pantry staple. Nothing could be more quick and easy — just stir couscous into boiling stock then let stand for 5 minutes and it's ready to serve. Generally, though, it's best when dressed up. Here, the tiny grains are infused with curry flavours, then tossed with chicken, cranberries and bell pepper.

1	cup (250 mL) plain yogurt
2	tablespoons (30 mL) mango chutney
¼	cup (50 mL) chopped fresh parsley
1¾	cups (425 mL) chicken stock
1	teaspoon (5 mL) medium-hot Indian curry paste
⅓	cup (75 mL) dried cranberries
1	tablespoon (15 mL) lemon juice
1½	cups (375 mL) couscous
1	tablespoon (15 mL) vegetable oil
1	pound (500 g) boneless skinless chicken thighs, cut into bite-size pieces
1	onion, chopped
1	large garlic clove, minced
1	red bell pepper, chopped coarse
	Salt and pepper

In small bowl, combine yogurt, chutney and parsley; set sauce aside.

In large saucepan, whisk together stock and curry paste; cover and bring to a boil. Stir in cranberries and lemon juice. Stir in couscous; cover and remove from heat. Let stand for 5 minutes. Fluff with fork and cover.

Meanwhile, heat oil in large heavy frypan over medium-high heat. Add chicken thighs and saute for 3 to 5 minutes or until cooked. Using slotted spoon, transfer chicken to bowl.

Reduce heat to medium. Add onion, garlic and red pepper to frypan; saute for 3 to 5 minutes or until vegetables are tender-crisp. Return chicken to frypan and heat through.

Fluff couscous again; add chicken mixture and stir to mix. Add salt and pepper to taste. Transfer to serving platter. Serve with yogurt chutney sauce. ↻

TIP: Dried cranberries are an ideal pantry item. Like most dried fruit, they quickly add intense flavour, and can be stored at room temperature, tightly wrapped in a plastic resealable bag, for up to 6 months.

Per serving:

544 calories, 38.2 g protein, 9.1 g fat, 75.5 g carbohydrate. Excellent source of vitamins B6, B12, C, riboflavin, niacin and folate. Excellent source of magnesium, phosphorus and zinc.

Curried Chicken Burgers

Makes 4 servings

Even the prosaic burger can flirt with fusion flavours. We developed this chicken burger enlisting two Indian heavyweight champions: curry paste and mango chutney. Amid all that heat, a cooling contrast is needed, and our first choice would be raita, a highly variable yogurt-based sauce, often seasoned with roasted cumin seeds and chopped fresh herbs. It frequently accompanies Indian curries. But it's difficult to find already made, so a similar sauce from Greece, tzatziki, makes a worthy stand-in. If you want to keep globetrotting, forget hamburger buns and pop the patties into pita halves. Try a cooling shredded carrot salad on the side.

1	pound (500 g) ground chicken
2	tablespoons (30 mL) dry bread crumbs
2	tablespoons (30 mL) mango chutney
1	tablespoon (15 mL) water
1	tablespoon (15 mL) plain yogurt
2	green onions, chopped
1	teaspoon (5 mL) hot Indian curry paste
1	teaspoon (5 mL) salt
2	(7-inch/18 cm) pita breads
	Leaf lettuce
1	tomato, sliced thin
½	cup (125 mL) purchased tzatziki

In bowl, combine ground chicken, bread crumbs, chutney, water, yogurt, green onions, curry paste and salt. Shape into 4 patties, about ¾-inch (2 cm) thick. Place on greased broiler pan and broil for 15 to 18 minutes or until no longer pink inside, turning once.

Cut each pita bread crosswise in half. Line each half with lettuce and a tomato slice, then tuck patty inside. Top each burger with 2 tablespoons (30 mL) tzatziki. ○

WHAT IS TZATZIKI?

This yogurt-based Greek sauce regularly accompanies the grilled skewered meats called souvlaki. It usually includes grated cucumber, garlic, lemon juice and dill or mint. Tzatziki is now sold in plastic tubs in the dairy case of many supermarkets.

Per serving:

303 calories, 32.5 g protein, 4.6 g fat, 31 g carbohydrate. Excellent source of vitamin B6 and niacin. Excellent source of zinc.

Chicken Lo Mein

Makes 4 servings

"Mein" means noodles in Chinese and "lo" means sprinkle. So "lo mein" is noodles sprinkled with various stir-fried ingredients. These noodles are mixed with chicken, red peppers and bok choy.

Noodles

1	(300 g) package Chinese-style fresh thin egg noodles
1	tablespoon (15 mL) sesame oil
1	tablespoon (15 mL) vegetable oil
1	tablespoon (15 mL) finely chopped fresh ginger
2	garlic cloves, minced
2	tablespoons (30 mL) chicken stock
¼	teaspoon (1 mL) salt

Stir-fry

4	small boneless skinless chicken breasts, cut into thin strips (about 1 pound/500 g total)
	Salt and pepper
1	tablespoon (15 mL) vegetable oil
1	red bell pepper, cut into 1-inch (2.5 cm) pieces
1	pound (500 g) baby bok choy, chopped coarse (about 10 cups/2.5 L)
½	cup (125 mL) chicken stock
½	teaspoon (2 mL) hot chili paste
½	cup (125 mL) finely chopped green onions

Noodles: Cook noodles in large pot of boiling salted water for 1 to 2 minutes or until tender. Drain and rinse with cold water; drain well. Put into large bowl and toss with sesame oil; set aside.

In large nonstick wok, heat vegetable oil over medium heat. Add ginger and garlic; stir-fry for 30 seconds. Add stock and salt; cook for 30 seconds. Transfer to bowl with noodles; toss and set aside.

Stir-fry: Lightly sprinkle chicken strips with salt and pepper. In wok, heat vegetable oil over medium-high heat. Add chicken and stir-fry for 3 minutes or until no longer pink inside. With slotted spoon, transfer chicken to bowl with noodles.

Add red pepper and bok choy to wok; stir-fry for 3 minutes or just until tender-crisp. Combine stock and chili paste; add to wok and cook for 1 minute. Add noodle mixture to wok and heat through. Stir in green onions, and salt and pepper to taste. Transfer to serving platter. ↻

TIPS

- We suggest you chop, mince and slice everything before starting to stir-fry — the cooking is done in stages and you move quickly from one to the next.

- If you like heat, increase the hot chili paste.

SUBSTITUTION: Use ½ pound (250 g) dried thin noodles such as angel hair pasta or Chinese-style wun tun noodles (not to be confused with wonton wrappers) instead of fresh noodles.

Per serving:

494 calories, 40 g protein, 14.9 g fat, 49.6 g carbohydrate. Excellent source of vitamins A, B6, B12, C, niacin and folate. Excellent source of magnesium, phosphorus and zinc.

EXTRA FAST

Farfalle with Chicken and Sugar Snap Peas

Makes 4 servings

We are partial to this neat and tidy pasta shape that looks like a little bow-tie. You may see packages that use the Italian term, farfalle (that's the plural of "butterfly," a pleasing image), while others call it "bow" or occasionally "bow-tie." Toss with sugar snap peas, chicken, mushrooms and baby spinach for an easy pasta dish that will please both family and guests.

4	cups (1 L) farfalle (medium-size bow pasta)
2	cups (500 mL) sugar snap peas
3	tablespoons (45 mL) olive oil, divided
2	small boneless skinless chicken breasts, cut into thin strips (½ pound/250 g total)
	Salt and pepper
1	onion, sliced thin
1	large garlic clove, minced
2	cups (500 mL) sliced mushrooms (6 ounces/170 g)
¼	teaspoon (1 mL) dried crushed hot red pepper
4	cups (1 L) lightly packed fresh baby spinach
2	tablespoons (30 mL) water
½	cup (125 mL) chopped fresh Italian (flat-leaf) parsley
½	cup (125 mL) grated parmesan cheese

Cook farfalle in large pot of boiling salted water until tender, adding peas during last 2 minutes of pasta cooking time; drain pasta and peas and return to pot. Add 1 tablespoon (15 mL) oil and toss.

Meanwhile, lightly sprinkle chicken with salt and pepper. In large heavy frypan, heat 1 tablespoon (15 mL) oil over medium-high heat. Add chicken, onion and garlic; saute for 3 to 5 minutes or until chicken is no longer pink inside. Transfer chicken mixture to bowl and keep warm.

Add remaining 1 tablespoon (15 mL) oil to frypan. Add mushrooms and dried red pepper; saute for 3 to 4 minutes or until mushrooms are tender. Add spinach and water; cook for 1 minute or until wilted, stirring constantly. Add to pasta mixture.

Add chicken mixture and parsley to pasta; toss. Add salt and pepper to taste. Transfer to serving platter. Sprinkle with parmesan cheese. ○

TIME SAVERS

- Purchase washed, ready-to-use, fresh stringless sugar snap peas: A 227 gram package yields about 2 cups (500 mL).

- Purchase washed, ready-to-use fresh baby spinach: A 170 gram package yields about 8 cups (2 L) lightly packed.

Per serving:

630 calories, 48.6 g protein, 17.5 g fat, 68.5 g carbohydrate. Excellent source of vitamins A, B6, C, niacin and folate. Excellent source of iron, zinc, magnesium and phosphorus. Very high in fibre.

Double Tomato Chicken Couscous

Makes 4 servings

The flavour of sun-dried tomato pesto pops out in a dish. In this one, it also gives the canned tomatoes more character. This mix of chicken, carrots and tomatoes sits atop a mound of lemony couscous — so simple to make and so good for you. If you have a Mediterranean-style deli nearby, pick up some dolmades or hummus with whole-wheat pita to start off the meal.

2	tablespoons (30 mL) olive oil, divided
4	small boneless skinless chicken breasts, cut into thin strips (about 1 pound/500 g total)
	Salt and pepper
2	cups (500 mL) thinly sliced carrots
1	onion, chopped
1	large garlic clove, minced
1	(540 mL) can tomatoes (undrained), chopped
1	tablespoon (15 mL) sun-dried tomato pesto
	Pinch dried crushed hot red pepper
1¾	cups (425 mL) chicken stock
1	tablespoon (15 mL) lemon juice
1½	cups (375 mL) couscous
¼	cup (50 mL) chopped fresh parsley

In large heavy frypan, heat 1 tablespoon (15 mL) oil over medium-high heat. Add chicken and saute for 3 to 4 minutes or until no longer pink inside. Transfer chicken and any juices to bowl. Lightly sprinkle with salt and pepper; set aside.

Add remaining 1 tablespoon (15 mL) oil to frypan and heat. Add carrots, onion and garlic; saute for 3 minutes. Add tomatoes, pesto and dried red pepper. Cover, reduce heat and simmer for 8 minutes or until carrots are tender-crisp.

Meanwhile, put stock in large saucepan; cover and bring to a boil. Stir in lemon juice, then couscous; cover and remove from heat. Let stand for 5 minutes. Fluff with fork and cover.

Return chicken to frypan and heat through. Add salt and pepper to taste.

Fluff couscous again; add parsley and stir to mix. Add salt and pepper to taste. Spoon couscous on to large deep serving platter and top with chicken mixture. ↻

TIP: Sun-dried tomato pesto, a fine convenience product, adds an intense heady flavour. It can be found both in the refrigerated fresh pasta section in most supermarkets and in shelf-stable jars.

TIME SAVER: Use scissors to chop canned tomatoes right in the can. You'll save a little time and a lot of cleanup.

Per serving:

566 calories, 41.1 g protein, 11.3 g fat, 73.7 g carbohydrate. Excellent source of vitamins A, B6, C, thiamin, niacin and folate. Excellent source of iron, magnesium and phosphorus. High in fibre.

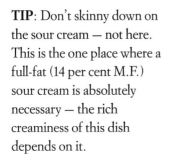

TIP: Don't skinny down on the sour cream — not here. This is the one place where a full-fat (14 per cent M.F.) sour cream is absolutely necessary — the rich creaminess of this dish depends on it.

One-Pot Creamy Noodles with Chicken and Broccoli

Makes 4 servings

Just one frypan is used to cook this luxurious dish. It's not only easy to make, but one-pot cooking makes clean up a breeze, too. Caesar salad makes a refreshing accompaniment, splashed with a bottled dressing.

2   tablespoons (30 mL) vegetable oil
4   small boneless skinless chicken breasts, cut into 1-inch (2.5 cm) pieces (about 1 pound/500 g total)
1   small onion, chopped
1   large garlic clove, minced
3   cups (750 mL) chicken stock
3   cups (750 mL) medium egg noodles
2   cups (500 mL) small broccoli florets
1   cup (250 mL) sour cream (14 per cent M.F.)
    Salt and pepper
    Chopped fresh parsley

In 11-inch (28 cm) heavy frypan, heat oil over medium-high heat. Add chicken pieces, onion and garlic; saute for 6 minutes or until chicken is no longer pink inside. Transfer chicken mixture to bowl and set aside.

Add stock to frypan. Cover and increase heat to high; bring to a boil. Add noodles and boil, uncovered, for 6 minutes, stirring occasionally. Add broccoli and reduce heat to medium; cover partially and cook for 2 to 3 minutes or until noodles are tender and broccoli is cooked, stirring occasionally. Remove about 2 tablespoons (30 mL) liquid from frypan and discard. Reduce heat to low. Stir in sour cream. Return chicken mixture to frypan; stir and heat through. Add salt and pepper to taste. Serve in pasta bowls garnished with parsley. ☉

Per serving:

431 calories, 36.8 g protein, 18.9 g fat, 27.1 g carbohydrate. Excellent source of vitamin C. Excellent source of magnesium and phosphorus.

EXTRA FAST

Spicy Noodles with Chicken and Cherry Tomatoes

Makes 4 servings

Rice noodles are a dream ingredient — cover them with boiling water and they quietly plump up into delicate strands. While that's happening, the cook has time to prepare a sauce and any other desired components for a fine stir-fry.

8	ounces (250 g) broad rice stick noodles
3	tablespoons (45 mL) ketjap manis
2	tablespoons (30 mL) dry sherry or dry white wine
1	teaspoon (5 mL) sambal oelek
3	small boneless skinless chicken breasts, cut into thin strips (about ¾ pound/350 g total)
2	tablespoons (30 mL) vegetable oil, divided
1	small onion, chopped coarse
2	garlic cloves, minced
1	tablespoon (15 mL) grated fresh ginger
½	pound (250 g) yard-long beans or thin green beans, cut into 2-inch (5 cm) pieces (2 cups/500 mL)
½	cup (125 mL) chicken stock
	Salt and pepper
2	cups (500 mL) cherry tomatoes, halved

Place noodles in 13x9-inch (33x23 cm) heatproof baking dish and cover with boiling water. Let stand for 25 minutes or until tender; drain.

Meanwhile, whisk together ketjap manis, sherry and sambal oelek in small bowl. Add chicken and marinate for 10 minutes.

In large nonstick wok, heat 1 tablespoon (15 mL) oil over medium-high heat. Add onion, garlic, ginger and beans; stir-fry for 4 minutes. Transfer bean mixture to large bowl; set aside.

Heat remaining 1 tablespoon (15 mL) oil in wok. Using slotted spoon, remove chicken from marinade and add to wok; reserve marinade. Stir-fry for 3 minutes or until chicken is no longer pink inside. Transfer chicken to bowl with bean mixture.

Add stock and reserved marinade to wok; bring to a boil and boil for 1 minute. Add drained noodles, cooked bean mixture, cooked chicken, and salt and pepper to taste; stir to combine. Add tomatoes and stir gently until just combined. Transfer to serving platter. ♂

WHAT IS KETJAP MANIS?

The Indonesian sweet sauce known as ketjap manis (or kecap manis) is a syrupy-thick, molasses-flavoured, dark soy sauce. (Our word "ketchup" is rooted here.) More complex in flavour than regular soy sauce, it's widely used in Malaysian and Indonesian cooking. Several brands are available in Asian stores and most large supermarkets — we like the Conimex brand from Holland.

STICK TO YOUR SIZE

Packaged, dried rice stick noodles are imported from China, Thailand and Vietnam, and come in various widths. We used the package labelled "large," with noodles about ¼-inch (5 mm) wide, for our stir-fry. Save the medium and small noodles for soup.

WHAT IS SAMBAL OELEK?

One tip that a dish will be spicy is "sambal" in the ingredient list. Sambal is a bright-red Indonesian hot sauce made with ground chilies (seeds included) that adds a fiery heat.

Per serving:

438 calories, 22.7 g protein, 8.5 g fat, 65.7 g carbohydrate. Excellent source of vitamins B6, C and niacin.

Pick-of-the-Garden Chicken Spaghetti

Makes 4 servings

For the family chef on the run, a quick, inspired meal is easily made if you reach for a jar of pasta sauce, and punch it up with fresh ingredients. We've boosted the flavour with onion, garlic and vegetables. This sauce tastes like you've hunkered over the stove for much longer than the 10 minutes it actually requires. Serve with a caesar salad and warm focaccia.

¾	**pound (350 g) spaghetti**
1	**tablespoon (15 mL) olive oil**
½	**pound (250 g) boneless skinless chicken thighs, cut into thin strips**
	Salt and pepper
1	**small onion, chopped**
2	**garlic cloves, minced**
½	**cup (125 mL) thinly sliced celery**
1	**small zucchini, diced**
1	**(700 mL) jar tomato-based pasta sauce**
1	**tomato, chopped**
¼	**cup (50 mL) chopped fresh parsley**
¼	**cup (50 mL) grated parmesan cheese**

Cook spaghetti in large pot of boiling salted water until tender; drain.

Meanwhile, heat oil in large heavy frypan over medium-high heat. Lightly sprinkle chicken strips with salt and pepper. Put chicken in frypan and saute for 2 to 3 minutes or until cooked. Using slotted spoon, transfer chicken to bowl.

Add onion and garlic to frypan; saute for 1 minute. Add celery and zucchini; saute for 2 to 3 minutes or until vegetables are tender. Reduce heat to medium-low and stir in pasta sauce; cook for 2 minutes or until heated through. Stir in tomato, parsley and chicken; cook for 1 minute.

Serve sauce over pasta. Sprinkle with parmesan cheese. ⊘

TIP: Jars of commercial tomato-based pasta sauce come in a range of sizes, while this recipe suggests using a 700 mL jar, that amount isn't crucial — choose a sauce you like in approximately that volume. When using bottled pasta sauce, add a chopped fresh ripe tomato and heat through — it will make the dish much more lively.

Per serving:

530 calories, 27.6 g protein, 8.9 g fat, 86.6 g carbohydrate. Excellent source of vitamins A, C and folate. Excellent source of iron.

Mango Chutney Turkey Feast

Makes 4 servings

Turkey has become an all-season staple of the poultry department, offering a welcome option that takes to a wide range of flavours. These cutlets take only five minutes to cook, and paired with a sweet-tart sauce made from pan juices, shallot, lime juice and mango chutney, they can easily be the centrepiece of elegant entertaining. Only the cook will know that the whole dish took less than 20 minutes to prepare. Aromatic basmati rice and a fresh green vegetable such as asparagus complement the turkey and add finesse to the plate.

1	pound (500 g) turkey breast cutlets
	Salt and pepper
1	tablespoon (15 mL) butter
1	tablespoon (15 mL) vegetable oil
1	large shallot, chopped fine
1	large garlic clove, minced
¼	cup (50 mL) chicken stock
¼	cup (50 mL) mango chutney
1	teaspoon (5 mL) hot Indian curry paste
2	teaspoons (10 mL) lime juice

Lightly sprinkle turkey cutlets with salt and pepper.

In large heavy frypan, heat butter and oil over medium-high heat. Add cutlets and saute for 5 minutes or until no longer pink inside, turning once. Transfer cutlets to plate and keep warm.

Reduce heat to medium. Add shallot and garlic to frypan; saute for 30 seconds. Add stock, stirring and scraping browned bits from bottom of frypan. Add chutney, curry paste and lime juice; cook for 1 minute, stirring occasionally. Add salt and pepper to taste. Transfer cutlets to serving platter. Pour sauce over cutlets. ◷

TIP: Bottled Indian curry pastes range from mild to extra-hot, and add flavour and depth without being too harsh. The blends usually contain ghee (clarified butter) and vinegar, plus spices selected from a wide, wide range. With many brands on the market with various heat levels, it's a matter of experimenting to settle on one you like. We find the pastes superior to curry powder, which can sometimes taste raw and dusty. We tested this recipe using Patak's Original curry paste, sold in 284 mL jars. Once opened, bottled paste will keep for up to 6 months in the refrigerator.

Per serving:

239 calories, 29.8 g protein, 8.4 g fat, 9.9 g carbohydrate. Excellent source of vitamin B6 and niacin.

Turkey Cutlets with Cran-Apple Sauce

Makes 4 servings

The combination of cranberry and apple evokes thoughts of special meals celebrated late in the year. Thanks to the intense flavour of dried cranberries, which are always available (and a valuable pantry item), this dish is do-able in any month. Serve with small red-skinned potatoes, seasonal vegetables and a crisp green salad.

1	pound (500 g) turkey breast cutlets
	Salt and pepper
1	tablespoon (15 mL) butter
1	tablespoon (15 mL) vegetable oil
½	cup (125 mL) chopped onion
1	large garlic clove, minced
¾	cup (175 mL) fresh apple juice
¼	cup (50 mL) dried cranberries
2	teaspoons (10 mL) sherry vinegar or red wine vinegar
1	teaspoon (5 mL) chopped fresh thyme

Lightly sprinkle turkey cutlets with salt and pepper.

In large heavy frypan, heat butter and oil over medium-high heat. Add cutlets and saute for 5 minutes or until no longer pink inside, turning once. Transfer cutlets to plate and keep warm.

Reduce heat to medium. Add onion and garlic to frypan; saute for 3 minutes or until onion is tender. Add apple juice, cranberries, vinegar, thyme and drained juices from cutlets; boil for 4 minutes or until reduced and slightly thickened, stirring constantly. Add salt and pepper to taste. Transfer cutlets to serving platter. Pour sauce over cutlets. ⟳

WHAT IS SWEET APPLE CIDER?

Non-alcoholic or "sweet" cider is the fresh pressed apple juice before fermentation (it's actually unsweetened); it becomes hard cider after fermentation, with a varying range of alcohol content. The sweet type can be found in 2 L jugs, refrigerated, in supermarkets. Smaller bottles are available at some coffee shops and health food stores.

SUBSTITUTION: Turkey steaks can be substituted for cutlets. If necessary, pound steaks between two layers of wax paper until about ¼-inch (5 mm) thick, and cook until no longer pink inside.

Per serving:

243 calories, 30 g protein, 8.4 g fat, 11.2 g carbohydrate. Excellent source of vitamin B6 and niacin.

Grilled Turkey-Vegetable Panini

Makes 4 servings

During outdoor cooking season, why not improve on the submarine or hero sandwich by grilling the filling, and the bread, too? The grill adds a little smoke flavour and crispness to it all. If you brush the bread with a mixture of garlic oil and parmesan cheese, then warm it alongside the turkey, the result is a grilled-cheese taste with a difference — this is definitely far more inviting than a cold turkey sandwich.

¾	**pound (350 g) turkey breast steaks**
	Salt and pepper
	Barbecue sauce
2	**yellow bell peppers, cut lengthwise into quarters**
2	**red onions, cut into ¼-inch (5 mm) thick slices**
	Purchased olive oil flavoured with garlic, or regular olive oil
2	**tablespoons (30 mL) grated parmesan cheese**
1	**baguette (20 inches/50 cm long and 3½ inches/9 cm wide)**
	Light mayonnaise
1	**large tomato, sliced thin**
	Lettuce

Pound turkey steaks until ¼-inch (5 mm) thick. Sprinkle lightly with salt and pepper. Brush lightly with barbecue sauce; set aside. Brush yellow peppers and onions with garlic oil; set aside.

In small bowl, combine 3 tablespoons (45 mL) garlic oil and parmesan cheese. Cut baguette in half lengthwise. Lightly brush each cut side with parmesan mixture.

Place yellow peppers and onions on greased barbecue grill over medium-high heat for 15 minutes or until tender, turning occasionally and brushing lightly with garlic oil. Remove vegetables from grill, and sprinkle with salt and pepper to taste; set aside.

Place turkey on grill and cook for 5 minutes or until no longer pink inside, turning once. About 2 minutes before turkey is cooked, place bread, cut side down, on grill and heat for 2 minutes or until lightly toasted. Remove turkey and bread from grill.

Spread mayonnaise on bread halves. Place turkey, in single layer, on 1 bread half, then top with onions, peppers, tomato and lettuce. Cover with remaining bread half. To serve, cut into 4 equal pieces.

SUBSTITUTION: A baguette is the long, narrow classic loaf of french bread. Properly made, it has a crisp golden crust that crackles slightly when bitten into, along with a supple, light, chewy interior. You could use a multigrain or sourdough version for this sandwich.

Per serving:

345 calories, 29.8 g protein, 5.6 g fat, 42.9 g carbohydrate. Excellent source of vitamins A, B6, B12, C and niacin. Excellent source of iron and phosphorus.

W HAT IS FOCACCIA?

This dimpled flatbread, similar in basic flavour to pizza crust, was traditionally brushed with olive oil, sprinkled with salt crystals and baked in a wood-burning oven. A whole focaccia can weigh several pounds, but it's usually cut into manageable pieces when sold. A variety of ingredients can be worked into the dough — olives, pancetta, sun-dried tomatoes, onions and herbs, to name a few. Usually less than 2 inches (5 cm) thick, it's well suited for sandwiches or burgers when split in half horizontally. Focaccia can be found in most supermarkets, Italian bakeries and many specialty shops, but if you can't find it, don't fret. Go to your favourite bakery and choose from today's delicious array of fresh rolls and buns. Try turkey burgers in crusty round hamburger buns, kaisers, Portuguese buns or sourdough buns flecked with herbs.

Mediterranean Turkey Burgers

Makes 4 servings

Burgers are a fine midweek answer to the what's-for-supper? conundrum.

Want a burger with a difference? This one made from ground turkey takes well to all sorts of flavour additions. Dress it up with the intense flavours of black olives and sun-dried tomatoes and you have a memorable burger — especially when you put it on toasted focaccia bread instead of the usual bun.

1	pound (500 g) ground turkey
2	tablespoons (30 mL) chopped pitted kalamata olives
2	tablespoons (30 mL) chopped, drained sun-dried tomatoes (packed in oil)
1	tablespoon (15 mL) dry bread crumbs
1	tablespoon (15 mL) lemon juice
2	garlic cloves, minced
¼	teaspoon (1 mL) salt
¼	teaspoon (1 mL) pepper
4	(4½-inch/11 cm) mini herb focaccia, cut in half horizontally
	Light mayonnaise
	Sliced sweet onion
	Sliced tomato

In bowl, combine ground turkey, olives, sun-dried tomatoes, bread crumbs, lemon juice, garlic, salt and pepper. Shape into 4 patties, about ¾-inch (2 cm) thick. Place on greased broiler pan and broil for 10 minutes or until no loner pink inside, turning once.

Place focaccia, cut side up, on baking sheet and broil for 1 minute or until lightly toasted.

Spread each bottom piece of focaccia with mayonnaise. Top with turkey burger, onion and tomato; cover with top piece of focaccia. ◑

Per serving:

329 calories, 25.7 g protein, 13.4 g fat, 25 g carbohydrate. Excellent source of niacin and zinc.

10-Minute Turkey Chili with Soy

Makes 4 servings

Can you really make chili from scratch in just 10 minutes? "From scratch" might be a slight stretch, but this high-speed chili uses only two canned items, and there's no dispute about its great flavour. And it's also a good way to add more soy to your diet. Serve with multigrain rolls and a crunchy Greek salad.

1	tablespoon (15 mL) vegetable oil
½	pound (250 g) ground turkey
1	small onion, chopped
½	small green bell pepper, chopped
1	large garlic clove, minced
1	(398 mL) can chili-style stewed tomatoes
1	(398 mL) can black soy beans, drained and rinsed

In large heavy saucepan, heat oil over medium-high heat. Add ground turkey, onion, green pepper and garlic; saute for 5 minutes or until turkey is cooked and onion is tender. Add tomatoes and cook for 2 minutes. Add beans and cook for 1 to 2 minutes or until heated through.

SUBSTITUTIONS

- Flavoured canned stewed tomatoes save time because they're already seasoned (though you can certainly add more seasoning to suit your own taste). If your pantry offers only regular stewed tomatoes, use 1 (398 mL) can of those and up the heat with chili powder to taste. Add the chili powder along with the turkey, onion, green pepper and garlic.

- If desired, regular canned black beans can be used in place of black soy beans.

Per serving:

256 calories, 21.7 g protein, 12.1 g fat, 18.1 g carbohydrate. Excellent source of vitamin C, niacin and folate. Excellent source of iron and magnesium. High in fibre.

It's a Wrap! With Turkey

Makes 4 servings

This recipe makes great use of leftover turkey, but cooked chicken will work as well. Tzatziki (Greek yogurt-cucumber dip) and prosciutto add extra measures of flavour. Serve with a bean salad such as one made with canned mixed beans, sliced celery and chopped red onion, and dress with a tangy vinaigrette — it will keep in the fridge for hours.

¼	**cup (50 mL) light mayonnaise**
¼	**cup (50 mL) purchased tzatziki**
½	**cup (125 mL) chopped red onion**
½	**cup (125 mL) chopped red bell pepper**
2	**cups (500 mL) shredded lettuce**
4	**(10-inch/25 cm) flour tortillas**
½	**pound (250 g) cooked turkey, cut into ½-inch (1 cm) strips**
	Salt and pepper
2	**ounces (60 g) thinly sliced prosciutto (Italian ham)**
12	**thin slices plum tomato**

In small bowl, combine mayonnaise and tzatziki. Stir in onion and red pepper; set aside.

For each turkey wrap: Place ½ cup (125 mL) lettuce in centre of tortilla in an oblong shape (about 2½-inches/6 cm wide), about 2 inches (5 cm) from sides. Top with ¼ of the turkey and sprinkle lightly with salt and pepper. Top with ¼ of the prosciutto and 3 tomato slices. Spoon ¼ of the mayonnaise mixture evenly over top. Fold bottom edge (side closest to you) up over filling. Fold sides in toward centre. Roll up to form a rectangular package. ↻

Per serving:

351 calories, 27.2 g protein, 12 g fat, 34.9 g carbohydrate. Excellent source of vitamins B6, C, thiamin and niacin. Excellent source of iron, zinc and phosphorous.

Rotini with Turkey Sausage, Spinach and Parmesan
Makes 4 servings

Turkey sausage comes in styles to suit both mild-mannered palates and those attuned to spicy action, so buy the kind that your family likes best. While the pasta cooks, the sauce comes together in a jiffy, flavours building in the frypan. Little more than a loaf of ciabatta or Italian crusty rolls is needed to round out the meal, but if you have a few minutes to spare, a salad of tomato, cucumber and sweet onion slices embellished with kalamata olives and chopped fresh Italian (flat-leaf) parsley makes a pleasing side dish.

- 4 cups (1 L) rotini
- 1 tablespoon (15 mL) vegetable oil
- ¾ pound (350 g) turkey sausages, casings removed
- 1 onion, chopped
- 1 garlic clove, minced
- ¾ cup (175 mL) chicken stock
- 1 teaspoon (5 mL) dried basil leaves
  Pinch dried crushed hot red pepper
- 8 cups (2 L) lightly packed fresh spinach
- ½ cup (125 mL) grated parmesan cheese
  Salt and pepper

Cook rotini in large pot of boiling salted water until tender; drain and return to pot.

Meanwhile, heat oil in large heavy frypan over medium-high heat. Add sausage and saute for 5 minutes or until cooked, stirring to break up sausage. With slotted spoon, transfer sausage to bowl and set aside.

Drain off all but 1 tablespoon (15 mL) fat from frypan. Add onion and garlic to frypan; saute for 3 minutes or until tender. Add stock, basil and dried red pepper; boil for 1 minute, stirring and scraping browned bits from bottom of pan. Add spinach and cook for 1 minute, stirring frequently.

Add spinach mixture and sausage to pasta; toss. Add parmesan cheese and toss. Add salt and pepper to taste. Transfer to serving platter. ⏲

CHECK THE HEAT

Turkey sausage varies considerably in seasoning — some can be mild, almost bland, while others contain carefully balanced herbs and assertive spices. Once you've sauteed the sausage meat in this recipe, taste some, and let the intensity of flavour and your heat gauge determine if you need to add more dried crushed hot red pepper.

Per serving:

574 calories, 35.3 g protein, 15.8 g fat, 72.2 g carbohydrate. Excellent source of vitamins A, B6, niacin and folate. Excellent source of magnesium and zinc. High in fibre.

Turkey Meatball Fettuccine

Makes 4 servings

TIP: Different shapes of
pasta suit different sauces.
Long pastas such as
fettuccine, linguine or
tagliatelle are ideal for this
recipe, with its heavier
tomato sauce. How do you
decide if it's a good marriage
of shape and sauce?
Generally, if all of the
ingredients will stick to long
pasta when it's twirled on a
fork (except of course
meatballs) it's suitable;
otherwise, serve the sauce
with stubby or short pasta.

*If you think spaghetti-and-meatballs is passé, think again. What was
once a popular but time-consuming '50s dish can now be prepared in
just a few minutes. Convenience items from the supermarket (tomato-
based pasta sauce, dry bread crumbs and freshly grated parmesan
cheese) make it easy.*

*For a change of pace, we make these meatballs with lean ground
turkey, and use fettuccine as the pasta.*

*As soon as you get in the door put the pasta water on to boil and
preheat the oven, then prepare the meatballs. Bake the meatballs while
the noodles cook and the bottled sauce heats. Serve with a green salad
of romaine lettuce, chopped fennel and diced red onions.*

½	**pound (250 g) ground turkey**
½	**pound (250 g) turkey sausages, casings removed**
2	**tablespoons (30 mL) dry bread crumbs**
1	**tablespoon (15 mL) water**
2	**green onions, chopped fine**
2	**teaspoons (10 mL) lemon juice**
½	**teaspoon (2 mL) salt**
¼	**teaspoon (1 mL) pepper**
¾	**pound (350 g) fettuccine**
1	**(700 mL) jar tomato-based pasta sauce**
¼	**cup (50 mL) grated parmesan cheese**

In medium bowl, combine ground turkey, sausage, bread
crumbs, water, green onions, lemon juice, salt and pepper.

Shape turkey mixture into 1½-inch (4 cm) meatballs; place on
wire rack in rimmed baking sheet. Bake at 450 F (230 C) for 10 to
12 minutes or until cooked.

Meanwhile, cook fettuccine in
large pot of boiling salted
water until tender; drain.

In large heavy saucepan,
heat pasta sauce; add
cooked meatballs. Serve
meatball sauce over pasta.
Sprinkle with
parmesan cheese. ⟳

Per serving:

616 calories, 37.4 g protein, 14 g fat,
84.1 g carbohydrate. Excellent source
of vitamins B6, B12, riboflavin and
niacin. Excellent source of iron, zinc,
magnesium and phosphorus.

Cranberry, Turkey and Spinach Couscous

Makes 4 servings

Once you get the hang of cooking couscous (and there's not much to it), you'll find it a quick shortcut to dinner. While the couscous and cranberries sit absorbing the hot chicken stock, saute the remaining ingredients in minutes. The sparks of fire from dried, crushed hot red peppers are countered by the mango chutney-yogurt mixture. This is a meal in itself; for a sweet finish serve fresh berries or slices of melon.

Yogurt chutney sauce

1	cup (250 mL) plain yogurt
¼	cup (50 mL) mango chutney

Couscous

1¾	cups (425 mL) chicken stock
	Pinch dried crushed hot red pepper
⅓	cup (75 mL) dried cranberries
2	tablespoons (30 mL) lemon juice
1	to 2 tablespoons (15 to 30 mL) chopped fresh sage
1½	cups (375 mL) couscous
2	tablespoons (30 mL) vegetable oil
1	onion, chopped
1	small red bell pepper, chopped coarse
3	cups (750 mL) cubed cooked turkey
1	cup (250 mL) shredded fresh spinach
	Salt and pepper

Yogurt chutney sauce: In small bowl, combine yogurt and chutney; set aside.

Couscous: In large saucepan, combine stock, dried red pepper and cranberries. Cover and place over high heat; bring to a boil. Stir in lemon juice and sage. Stir in couscous; cover and let stand for 5 minutes. Fluff with fork and cover.

Meanwhile, heat oil in large heavy frypan over medium-high heat. Add onion and saute for 1 minute. Add red bell pepper and saute for 2 minutes or until vegetables are almost tender. Add turkey and heat through, about 1 minute. Stir in spinach until just wilted. Add salt and pepper to taste.

Fluff couscous again; add turkey mixture and stir to mix. Add salt and pepper to taste. Transfer to serving platter. Serve with yogurt chutney sauce. ↻

TIPS

• Use dark or white cooked turkey meat. If you have cooked pork or chicken on hand, either would also work well.

• Other dried fruit such as blueberries, cherries, currants or golden raisins could be used.

Per serving:

574 calories, 45.8 g protein, 11.5 g fat, 70.2 g carbohydrate. Excellent source of vitamins A, B6, B12, C, riboflavin, niacin and folate. Excellent source of magnesium.

Turkey Tortelloni with Mushrooms and Bell Pepper

Makes 4 servings

Tortelloni look like tortellini that have been spending time at the gym – they're bigger, pumped up. Of course, if you prefer the smaller form of filled pastas, they'll work just as well. While the turkey tortelloni boils, and the sauce heats, you can quickly saute the onion, bell pepper and zucchini to toss with the pasta. Try this with a salad of romaine, avocado slices and grapefruit sections.

1	(350 g) package fresh turkey tortelloni
2	cups (500 mL) bottled tomato-based pasta sauce
1	tomato, chopped coarse
2	tablespoons (30 mL) vegetable oil
1	small onion, chopped
2	cups (500 mL) sliced mushrooms (about 6 ounces/170 g)
1	small yellow bell pepper, sliced
1	small zucchini, sliced
	Salt and pepper
2	tablespoons (30 mL) grated parmesan cheese

Cook tortelloni in large pot of boiling salted water according to package directions; drain and return to pot.

Meanwhile, put pasta sauce and tomato in medium-size heavy saucepan. Place over medium heat until heated through, stirring occasionally; keep warm.

Meanwhile, heat oil in large heavy frypan over medium-high heat. Add onion and saute for 2 minutes. Add mushrooms and saute for 2 minutes. Add yellow pepper and saute for 1 minute. Add zucchini and saute for 2 minutes or until vegetables are tender. Add salt and pepper to taste. Add vegetables to tortelloni and toss. Transfer to serving platter and top with pasta sauce. Sprinkle with parmesan cheese. ⟳

SUBSTITUTION: For a vegetarian version, use a cheese- or vegetable-filled tortelloni.

Per serving:

401 calories, 16.7 g protein, 13.6 g fat, 56 g carbohydrate. Excellent source of vitamin C and folate. Excellent source of phosphorus. High in fibre.

Roast Turkey with Cranberry-Raspberry Sauce

Makes 4 servings

What's roast turkey doing in a fast-meal cookbook? Good question, easily answered. Because turkey-with-cranberries is always a treat, we wanted a version that's quick to prepare. Here it is. The secret to its speed lies in using frozen cranberry-raspberry cocktail as the base for a sauce. It gives the turkey breast a beautiful lift.

1   **tablespoon (15 mL) vegetable oil**
1   **(1-pound/500 g) boneless skinless turkey breast**
     Salt and pepper
3   **tablespoons (45 mL) frozen cranberry-raspberry cocktail concentrate (undiluted), thawed**
1   **tablespoon (15 mL) balsamic vinegar**
1   **teaspoon (5 mL) vegetable oil**
1   **shallot, chopped fine**
1   **garlic clove, minced**
2   **tablespoons (30 mL) canned chicken broth (undiluted)**

Preheat oven to 400 F (200 C).

In 9-inch (23 cm) heavy frypan, heat 1 tablespoon (15 mL) oil over medium-high heat. Lightly sprinkle turkey breast with salt and pepper. Add turkey to frypan and cook for 4 minutes, turning once.

Meanwhile, stir together cranberry-raspberry cocktail, vinegar and 1 teaspoon (5 mL) oil; remove 1 tablespoon (15 mL) and set aside for brushing turkey. Reserve remainder for making sauce.

Remove frypan from heat and transfer browned turkey breast to baking pan. (Don't clean frypan.) Lightly brush turkey with some of the 1 tablespoon (15 mL) cranberry-raspberry mixture and put in oven for 15 to 20 minutes or until no longer pink inside, lightly brushing twice with remaining cranberry-raspberry mixture.

About 5 minutes before turkey is done, prepare sauce. Place same frypan over medium-low heat, adding a little extra oil if necessary. Add shallot and garlic; saute for 2 minutes or until tender. Add reserved cranberry-raspberry mixture and chicken broth; boil gently for 2 minutes or until slightly thickened, stirring and scraping browned bits from bottom of pan. Add salt and pepper to taste.

Cut turkey into thin slices and place on serving platter. Pour sauce over turkey. ↺

TIP: If you're just in from work and would still like to make this recipe, you can thaw the frozen cranberry-raspberry cocktail by removing 3 tablespoons (45 mL) and spooning it into a Pyrex measuring cup or ramekin. Microwave on High for 15 seconds or until melted.

Per serving:

206 calories, 30.8 g protein, 5.4 g fat, 6.7 g carbohydrate. Excellent source of vitamins B6, B12 and niacin.

Grilled Turkey Breast with Lemon and Rosemary
Makes 4 servings

TIP: Select lemons that are firm and heavy for their size, with unblemished skin. Store for up to 1 week at room temperature or up to 3 weeks in the refrigerator. Large, rough-skinned lemons are best for grating. If a recipe calls for both grated lemon zest (the yellow part of the peel) and juice, it's far easier to grate first, then juice. When grating a lemon, make only one or two passes across the same patch of peel, otherwise you risk getting some of the bitter white pith below the surface.

The classic Mediterranean combination of rosemary and lemon works gently with turkey breast, adding deliciously clear accents without overpowering the poultry. This goes well with nugget potatoes (sprinkle on some parsley) and grilled asparagus.

1	(1-pound/500 g) boneless skinless turkey breast
	Salt and pepper
2	tablespoons (30 mL) olive oil
¾	teaspoon (4 mL) grated lemon zest
1	tablespoon (15 mL) fresh lemon juice
3	garlic cloves, minced
1	tablespoon (15 mL) finely chopped fresh rosemary

Pound turkey breast until about 1-inch (2.5 cm) thick. Sprinkle lightly with salt and pepper.

In small bowl, combine oil, lemon zest and juice, garlic, rosemary and ¼ teaspoon (1 mL) each of salt and pepper; mix well.

Brush 1 side of turkey with half the oil mixture. Place on greased barbecue grill, brushed side down, over medium-high heat; brush top with remaining oil mixture. Close lid and cook for 7 minutes; turn turkey over, close lid and cook for another 6 to 8 minutes or until no longer pink inside.

To serve, cut turkey into thin slices and place on serving platter. Season with salt and pepper to taste.

Per serving:

200 calories, 30.8 g protein, 7.7 g fat, 0.3 g carbohydrate. Excellent source of vitamins B6, B12 and niacin.

Smoked Turkey Pizza with Marinated Artichokes

Makes 4 to 6 servings

*Artichokes are one of **those** ingredients — you either love them or hate them. If you fall into the latter category, just omit them from this pizza — it's delicious with or without them. If you have some ham in the fridge, it could easily pinch-hit for the smoked turkey.*

2	cups (500 mL) grated provolone cheese
1	cup (250 mL) grated old white cheddar cheese
2	(12-inch/30 cm) purchased, prebaked thin pizza crusts
3	teaspoons (15 mL) olive oil
1	large jalapeno pepper, seeded and chopped fine
6	ounces (170 g) thinly sliced smoked turkey, cut into thin strips
½	cup (125 mL) thinly sliced red onion
½	small red bell pepper, julienned
1	(170 mL) jar marinated artichoke hearts, drained and chopped coarse
	Black pepper
¼	cup (50 mL) chopped fresh parsley

In bowl, combine provolone and cheddar cheeses; toss to mix.

For each pizza: Brush pizza crust with 1½ teaspoons (7 mL) oil, leaving ½-inch (1 cm) border. Sprinkle with ¾ cup (175 mL) cheese mixture.

Sprinkle with half the jalapeno pepper. Top with half the turkey, onion, red pepper and artichokes. Sprinkle with ¾ cup (175 mL) cheese mixture. Bake at 450 F (230 C) for 8 to 10 minutes or until cheese is melted and toppings are hot. Sprinkle lightly with black pepper. Sprinkle with half the parsley. ○

CHEESE PLEASE

Although cheese isn't an essential ingredient in pizzas, most contain some, and it's usually mozzarella. Other good melting cheeses such as provolone, fontina, swiss and monterey jack can be substituted for the mild, delicate mozzarella. Dry cheeses such as feta, romano or parmesan don't work well as the dominant cheese, but they can be mixed with other easy-melting cheeses to make a more intensely flavoured pizza.

Per serving:

1,000 calories, 46.4 g protein, 35.2 g fat, 123 g carbohydrate. Excellent source of vitamin B12, thiamin, riboflavin, niacin and folate. Excellent source of calcium, iron, zinc, magnesium and phosphorus. High in fibre.

CHAPTER THREE

SEAFOOD

*Ruling a big country is like
cooking a small fish.
Too much handling will spoil it.*

Lao-tzu, 550 BC

Cod Soup with Orzo and Fresh Basil

Makes 4 servings

Light, lean and mild-flavoured, cod lets other ingredients share its spotlight. In this soup, basil, garlic and tomatoes add distinctive notes to a base given heft by orzo, the tiny pasta. In Italian, orzo on its own means "barley," but the term is apt for the grain-shaped pasta. White wine lifts this soup a notch above comfort food. Round out the meal with an antipasto plate of marinated olives and grilled vegetables from the deli. Serve with wedges of herb focaccia.

2	tablespoons (30 mL) olive oil
1	onion, chopped
3	garlic cloves, minced
3	carrots, diced
4	cups (1 L) chicken stock
1	(796 mL) can stewed tomatoes
¼	cup (50 mL) dry white wine
½	cup (125 mL) orzo (rice-shaped pasta)
1	pound (500 g) cod fillets, cut into 1-inch (2.5 cm) pieces
2	tablespoons (30 mL) chopped fresh basil
	Salt and pepper
	Chopped fresh parsley

In large heavy saucepan, heat oil over medium-high heat. Add onion, garlic and carrots; saute for 5 minutes or until onion is tender. Add stock, tomatoes and wine; bring to a boil. Add orzo; reduce heat and simmer for 10 minutes. Add cod and basil; simmer for 4 minutes or until fish flakes easily when tested with a fork. Add salt and pepper to taste. Just before serving, sprinkle with parsley. ◐

LOWDOWN ON LEFTOVER WINE

A few lingering ounces of last night's dinner wine are ideal for adding flavour without much effort, but it's a shame to open a new bottle for just a few spoonfuls. If you're not into imbibing or the fridge doesn't harbour leftovers, keep some vermouth handy as a substitute (it keeps longer than table wine).

Per serving:

313 calories, 27.1 g protein, 8.3 g fat, 32.5 g carbohydrate. Excellent source of vitamins A, B6, B12, C and niacin. Excellent source of magnesium and phosphorus. High in fibre.

West Coast Salmon Chowder

Makes 4 servings

Let the French enjoy their bouillabaisse, the Italians their zuppa di pesce — on the Pacific Coast we sing the praises of salmon chowder, especially one that's quick to prepare. With the clock running on meal prep, instant potato flakes come to the rescue, thickening the soup effortlessly. You don't need anything more than chewy, buttered Portuguese rolls or baguette to complete this chill-chasing meal.

1	tablespoon (15 mL) vegetable oil
1	onion, chopped
2	stalks celery, chopped
4	cups (1 L) fish stock
3	cups (750 mL) milk
¾	pound (350 g) skinless salmon fillet, cut into 1-inch (2.5 cm) pieces
1½	cups (375 mL) instant potato flakes
½	teaspoon (2 mL) finely grated lemon zest
1	teaspoon (5 mL) salt
½	teaspoon (2 mL) pepper
2	tablespoons (30 mL) chopped fresh parsley
1	green onion, sliced thin

In large heavy saucepan, heat oil over medium-high heat. Add chopped onion and celery; saute for 5 minutes or until tender. Add stock and milk; bring just to a boil. Add salmon, reduce heat and simmer for 3 to 5 minutes or just until fish flakes easily when tested with a fork. Remove from heat and stir in potato flakes, lemon zest, salt and pepper; heat until hot and slightly thickened. Stir in parsley and green onion. ☉

Oh My! Thai Seafood Soup

Makes 4 servings

A lovely, aromatic soup designed to seduce the seafood lover. Cod, mussels and prawns luxuriate in coconut milk and chicken stock; turmeric turns it all sunset golden.

6½	ounces (200 g) cellophane (bean thread) noodles
1	tablespoon (15 mL) vegetable oil
⅓	cup (75 mL) minced shallots (about 2 ounces/60 g)
3	garlic cloves, minced
2	tablespoons (30 mL) grated fresh ginger
3	Thai red peppers, seeded and minced (1 teaspoon/5 mL)
1½	teaspoons (7 mL) turmeric
3	cups (750 mL) chicken stock
1	(400 mL) can coconut milk, stirred
1	teaspoon (5 mL) finely grated lime zest
2	tablespoons (30 mL) lime juice
½	pound (250 g) cod fillets, cut into 1-inch (2.5 cm) pieces
16	mussels, scrubbed and debearded
16	shelled raw prawns, deveined
	Salt and pepper
1	cup (250 mL) bean sprouts
2	tablespoons (30 mL) chopped fresh cilantro
2	green onions, julienned

Bring large pot of water to a boil; remove from heat. Add noodles and let soak for 10 minutes or until tender; drain and set aside.

Meanwhile, heat oil in large nonstick wok or frypan over medium-high heat. Add shallots, garlic, ginger, Thai peppers and turmeric; saute for 3 minutes, stirring constantly. Add stock, coconut milk, lime zest and lime juice. Bring to a boil, reduce heat and simmer for 3 minutes. Add cod, mussels and prawns; increase heat and simmer for 5 minutes or until seafood is cooked (prawns are pink, mussels are open and cod can be easily flaked with a fork). Discard any mussels that do not open. Add salt and pepper to taste.

To serve, place an equal portion of noodles and bean sprouts in each of 4 bowls. Top each serving with an equal portion of seafood and stock mixture. Garnish with cilantro and green onions. ☺

TIPS

• Use regular coconut milk in this soup; light coconut milk will curdle slightly. Do not confuse cream of coconut with coconut milk. (Cream of coconut is used in desserts and mixed drinks.)

• Slender Thai red peppers measure up to 2 inches (5 cm) long. Handle them with care — their volatile oils irritate the skin. Never touch your face or eyes when handling them (the burning oils aren't always completely removed by rinsing your hands). If possible, wear rubber gloves when handling hot peppers. Thai peppers can be scorching; if you prefer less heat, use the milder serranos or jalapenos.

Per serving:
530 calories, 25.1 g protein, 25.7 g fat, 52.6 g carbohydrate. Excellent source of vitamins B6, B12, C, niacin and folate. Excellent source of iron, magnesium and phosphorus.

Speedy Snapper Soup

Makes 4 servings

TIP: Seasoned canned
stewed tomatoes make a
terrific shortcut to robust
flavour.

*When time constraints rule out a lavish supper, that's still no reason
to wait in line at your neighbourhood fast-food outlet. Choose, instead,
this snapper soup, loaded with fresh vegetables. Soups are both simple to
make and an enduringly popular way to enjoy the flavours of the sea. As
always, the fresher the fish, the better the dish. And don't forget a crusty
loaf — what's good soup without good bread?*

1	tablespoon (15 mL) vegetable oil
1	small onion, chopped
2	carrots, diced
2	stalks celery, sliced
3	cups (750 mL) chicken stock
2	(398 mL) cans Italian-style stewed tomatoes
1	large potato, cut into 1-inch (2.5 cm) pieces
1	pound (500 g) snapper fillets, cut into 1-inch (2.5 cm) pieces
2	cups (500 mL) coarsely chopped fresh spinach
¼	cup (50 mL) chopped fresh parsley
	Salt and pepper

In large heavy saucepan, heat oil over medium-high heat. Add
onion, carrots and celery; saute for 4 minutes or until onion is
tender. Add stock, tomatoes and potato. Bring to a boil over high
heat. Reduce heat and simmer, covered, for 10 minutes or until
potatoes are almost tender. Add snapper and simmer, uncovered,
for 3 minutes. Stir in spinach and parsley; cook for 2 minutes or
until fish flakes easily when tested with a fork. Add salt and pepper
to taste. ○

SUBSTITUTION: Choose
your favourite white fish,
such as cod or halibut, in
place of snapper.

Per serving:

306 calories, 34.1 g protein, 6.8 g fat,
28.7 g carbohydrate. Excellent source
of vitamins A, B6, B12, C, niacin and
folate. Excellent source of iron,
magnesium and phosphorus. High in
fibre.

Fennel, Black Bean and Tuna Soup with Fresh Herbs

Makes 4 servings

Canned tuna has shed its dowdy image as a casserole ingredient and now teams up with new flavour partners. Here the old kitchen staple is combined with fennel, clam nectar and black beans for a light, healthful, comforting meal. Round out the main course with some thick slices of flaxseed bread and store-bought roasted red pepper dip.

2	tablespoons (30 mL) olive oil
1	small fennel bulb, chopped
1	small onion, chopped
2	garlic cloves, minced
1	(796 mL) can stewed tomatoes
1	(398 mL) can clam nectar
1	(540 mL) can black beans, drained and rinsed
1	(170 g) can solid white tuna (packed in water), drained and separated into small chunks
½	cup (125 mL) chopped fresh parsley
1	tablespoon (15 mL) chopped fresh basil
1	tablespoon (15 mL) chopped fresh oregano
	Salt and pepper

In large heavy saucepan, heat oil over medium heat. Add fennel, onion and garlic; saute for 10 minutes or until vegetables are tender and light golden.

Add tomatoes and clam nectar to fennel mixture. Bring to a boil; add beans, tuna, parsley, basil and oregano. Reduce heat and simmer for 2 minutes or until heated through. Add salt and pepper to taste. ⏱

WHAT IS FENNEL?

Widely available yet under-used, this somewhat strange-looking bulbous green cousin to celery goes by many names: anise, fennel bulb, florence fennel, sweet fennel and, in Italian neighbourhoods, finocchio. To prepare fennel, remove stalks, fronds and any brown outer leaves. (Fronds can be used as an anise-flavoured herb.) Cut fennel in half or quarters depending on size and cut into slices. Raw or cooked, fennel contributes a delicate, slightly sweet licorice taste to dishes. Avoid buying fennel with flowering fronds — it's old.

Per serving:

318 calories, 20.9 g protein, 8.2 g fat, 42.6 g carbohydrate. Excellent source of vitamins B6, B12, thiamin, niacin and folate. Excellent source of iron, zinc, magnesium and phosphorous. Very high in fibre.

EXTRA FAST

Grilled Salmon with Mango-Raspberry Spinach Salad

Makes 4 servings

Yum! Salmon. Mango. Raspberry. Are you hooked yet? This dish comes together in a flash, but don't restrict it to a workday family supper — it has entertainment potential, especially during grilling season. Invite friends and dazzle them with this eye-catching meal. The freshness of the salad brings out the best in salmon. And since the fire is lit, grill some vegetables, too: portobello mushrooms or red peppers. In foul weather, cook the salmon in a stovetop grill pan or under the broiler.

½	cup (125 mL) raspberry vinaigrette (purchased or home-made)
2	tablespoons (30 mL) finely chopped shallot
4	(1-inch/2.5 cm) salmon steaks, about 6 ounces (170 g) each
	Salt and pepper
1	red onion, cut into ¼-inch (5 mm) thick slices
8	cups (2 L) lightly packed fresh baby spinach
1	mango, sliced thin
1	cup (250 mL) raspberries, optional

In small bowl, combine vinaigrette and shallot. Divide mixture in half. Reserve half to toss with salad; use remaining half during grilling.

Lightly sprinkle salmon steaks with salt and pepper. Skewer onion slices with toothpicks so they don't fall apart on the grill. Brush one side of steaks and onion slices with some of the vinaigrette reserved for grilling. Place steaks and onions, brushed side down, on greased barbecue grill over medium-high heat. Brush top of steaks and onion slices with remaining vinaigrette reserved for grilling. Cook for 10 minutes or until fish flakes easily when tested with a fork and onion is tender-crisp, turning once.

In large bowl, toss together spinach, mango and raspberries. Add grilled onion and reserved vinaigrette; toss. Place an equal portion of salad on each of 4 plates. Top each with a salmon steak. ⏱

Note: A 170 gram package of washed, ready-to-use fresh baby spinach yields about 8 cups (2 L) lightly packed.

RASPBERRY VINAIGRETTE

1	cup (250 mL) raspberries
6	tablespoons (90 mL) white balsamic vinegar
2	tablespoons (30 mL) liquid honey
1	teaspoon (5 mL) dijon mustard
½	teaspoon (2 mL) salt
¼	teaspoon (1 mL) pepper
1	cup (250 mL) vegetable oil
¼	cup (50 mL) finely chopped shallots

Puree raspberries in blender; pour through sieve to remove seeds.

In bowl, whisk together puree, vinegar, honey, mustard, salt and pepper. Gradually whisk in oil; stir in shallots.

Makes about 2 cups (500 mL). You'll only need ½ cup (125 mL) for the salmon salad; refrigerate remaining vinaigrette for another use.

Per serving:

459 calories, 35.8 g protein, 27.8 g fat, 17.3 g carbohydrate. Excellent source of vitamins A, B12, C, thiamin, riboflavin, niacin and folate. Excellent source of magnesium and phosphorus. High in fibre.

Shrimp Noodle Salad

Makes 4 servings

Toss a riot of flavours into Chinese noodles — shrimp (fresh, please), bright vegetables, peanuts — then overlay all with an Asian dressing of your choice, but preferably one with a bite of chili pepper. This salad is as great looking as it is tasty — and no one will guess it isn't a home-made dressing. It makes a light meal on its own.

½	**pound (250 g) asparagus, trimmed**
1	**(300 g) package Chinese-style fresh thin egg noodles or ½ pound (250 g) dried thin egg noodles**
1	**red bell pepper, julienned**
½	**cup (125 mL) chopped green onions**
¼	**English cucumber, halved lengthwise and sliced thin (1 cup/250 mL)**
½	**pound (250 g) peeled cooked shrimp**
½	**cup (125 mL) coarsely chopped fresh cilantro or Italian (flat-leaf) parsley, divided**
½	**cup (125 mL) coarsely chopped roasted unsalted peanuts, divided**
1	**cup (250 mL) Asian-style salad dressing (purchased or home-made)**
	Salt and pepper

Diagonally cut asparagus into thin slices.

Cook fresh noodles and asparagus in large pot of boiling salted water for 2 minutes. (If using dried noodles, prepare according to package directions, adding asparagus for the last 2 minutes of noodle cooking time.) Drain, and rinse noodles and asparagus with cold water; drain well and put in large bowl.

Add red pepper, green onions, cucumber, shrimp, ¼ cup (50 mL) cilantro and ¼ cup (50 mL) chopped peanuts to noodles. Add dressing, and salt and pepper to taste; toss until combined. Transfer to serving platter. Sprinkle with remaining cilantro and nuts. ⟳

Note: Refrigerated bottled dressings have come a long way, so don't be afraid to try some of the newer ones. We used Renee's Japanese dressing.

ASIAN-STYLE DRESSING

3	**tablespoons (45 mL) mirin (sweet Japanese rice wine)**
2	**tablespoons (30 mL) sesame oil**
3	**tablespoons (45 mL) soy sauce**
1	**tablespoon (15 mL) finely chopped fresh ginger**
3	**tablespoons (45 mL) lime juice**
¼	**cup (50 mL) finely chopped shallot**
1	**small garlic clove, minced**
¾	**teaspoon (4 mL) hot chili paste**
1¼	**teaspoons (6 mL) granulated sugar**

In small bowl, whisk together all ingredients. Makes about 1 cup (250 mL).

Per serving:
621 calories, 24.3 g protein, 46.4 g fat, 31.8 g carbohydrate. Excellent source of vitamin B12, niacin and folate. Excellent source of iron, zinc and magnesium. High in fibre.

Lentil and Mixed-Bean Salmon Salad

Makes 4 servings

LEMON-HERB VINAIGRETTE

⅓   **cup (75 mL) olive oil**

1   **teaspoon (5 mL) grated lemon zest**

1   **tablespoon (15 mL) lemon juice**

1   **large garlic clove, minced**

3   **tablespoons (45 mL) chopped fresh parsley**

½   **teaspoon (2 mL) sherry vinegar or red wine vinegar**

1   **tablespoon (15 mL) grated parmesan cheese**

¾   **teaspoon (4 mL) salt**

½   **teaspoon (2 mL) pepper**

In small bowl, whisk together all ingredients. Makes about ½ cup (125 mL).

The can-opener is a perfectly respectable piece of kitchen equipment, and reaching for a can or two often saves the cook's sanity at meal time. This salad is a testament to healthy eating and it takes full advantage of pantry staples. The mixed beans we used included chickpeas, black-eyed peas, red kidney beans and romano beans. The vinaigrette will make a big difference to the taste, so if you don't make your own, buy one you know and like. Canned pink salmon works well, or splurge and substitute sockeye.

1   small red onion

1   small red bell pepper, chopped coarse

1   (540 mL) can mixed beans, drained and rinsed

1   (540 mL) can lentils, drained and rinsed

⅓   cup (75 mL) chopped fresh parsley

½   cup (125 mL) herb vinaigrette (purchased or home-made)

1   tablespoon (15 mL) lemon juice, optional

1   (213 g) can pink salmon, drained and separated into small chunks

   Lettuce

Cut onion in half lengthwise, then cut each half crosswise into thin slices. In large bowl, combine onion, red pepper, beans, lentils and parsley. Add vinaigrette and stir to mix. Taste and sprinkle with optional lemon juice, if desired. Gently toss in salmon chunks.

Line serving platter with lettuce and top with salmon mixture. ⏱

Note: If using purchased vinaigrette, taste salad before adding optional lemon juice — depending on the flavour of the vinaigrette you have chosen, it may be tangy enough.

Per serving:
460 calories, 24.5 g protein, 21.1 g fat, 45.7 g carbohydrate. Excellent source of vitamins B12, C, niacin and folate. Excellent source of iron, zinc and magnesium. Very high in fibre.

Any-Way-You-Like-It Tuna-and-Orzo Salad

Makes 4 servings

Hot or cold? The serving temperature of this salad can be the inverse of the temperature outside. On a warm day, take some big ruffled lettuce leaves and lounge this salad lazily on top. Complete the meal with a cheese plate and sliced baguette. On a cold day, enjoy it warm, with those Italian toasts called bruschetta, rubbed with a clove of garlic and brushed with extra-virgin olive oil.

1⅓   **cups (325 mL) orzo (rice-shaped pasta)**
2   **cups (500 mL) sugar snap peas**
1   **(170 g) can solid white tuna (packed in water), drained and separated into small chunks**
1   **(170 mL) jar marinated artichoke hearts, drained and chopped coarse**
¼   **cup (50 mL) pitted kalamata olives, halved**
1   **(398 mL) can red kidney beans, drained and rinsed**
2   **cups (500 mL) cherry tomatoes, halved (about ¾ pound/350 g)**
½   **cup (125 mL) herb vinaigrette (purchased or home-made)**
    Salt and pepper

Cook orzo in large pot of boiling salted water until tender, adding sugar snap peas for the last minute of pasta cooking time; drain. (If you're planning to serve the salad cold, rinse pasta and peas under cold running water; drain well.)

Meanwhile, combine tuna, artichoke hearts, olives, beans and tomatoes in large bowl. Add pasta (hot or cold), peas (hot or cold), vinaigrette, and salt and pepper to taste; toss. Transfer to serving platter. ○

Note: There are now many brands of bottled vinaigrette to choose from — some better than others. It's worth trying a few in small quantities to find one you like.

HERBED DIJON VINAIGRETTE

⅓   **cup (75 mL) olive oil**
2   **tablespoons (30 mL) white wine vinegar**
2   **teaspoons (10 mL) dijon mustard**
1   **garlic clove, minced**
1   **shallot, chopped fine**
2   **tablespoons (30 mL) chopped fresh basil**
½   **teaspoon (2 mL) salt**
¼   **teaspoon (1 mL) pepper**

In small bowl, whisk together all ingredients. Makes about ½ cup (125 mL).

TIME SAVER: Purchase washed, ready-to-use, fresh stringless sugar snap peas: A 227 gram package yields about 2 cups (500 mL).

Per serving:
457 calories, 22.4 g protein, 20.3 g fat, 48.6 g carbohydrate. Excellent source of vitamins B6, B12, C, thiamin, riboflavin, niacin and folate. Excellent source of iron, magnesium and phosphorus. Very high in fibre.

Grilled Salmon Fillets with Cranberry-Caper Vinaigrette

Makes 6 servings

This fine dish came to our kitchen from Daryle Nagata, executive chef at the Fairmont Waterfront Hotel in Vancouver.

Grill tender asparagus stalks along with the salmon, and serve with a squeeze of lemon.

Vinaigrette

½	cup (125 mL) red wine vinegar
¼	cup (50 mL) vegetable oil
¼	cup (50 mL) water
2	tablespoons (30 mL) drained capers
1	tablespoon (15 mL) finely chopped shallot
1	teaspoon (5 mL) chopped fresh chives
½	teaspoon (2 mL) chopped fresh thyme
½	teaspoon (2 mL) pink peppercorns
¼	teaspoon (1 mL) cayenne pepper
1	large garlic clove, minced
	Salt and pepper
¼	cup (50 mL) dried cranberries
6	lemon sections
6	lime sections

Salmon

6	salmon fillets (skin on), about 6 ounces (170 g) each
	Vegetable oil
	Salt and pepper

Vinaigrette: In bowl, whisk together vinegar, oil, water, capers, shallot, chives, thyme, peppercorns, cayenne pepper and garlic. Add salt and pepper to taste. Stir in cranberries, and lemon and lime sections. Just before serving, put vinaigrette in small saucepan and place over medium heat until just warm.

Salmon: Lightly brush salmon fillets with oil. Lightly sprinkle with salt and pepper. Place, skin side up, on greased barbecue grill over medium-high heat and cook for 10 minutes per inch (2.5 cm) of thickness or until fish flakes easily when tested with a fork, turning once. Pour some warm cranberry vinaigrette over each fillet. ⟳

MAKE AHEAD: The cranberry vinaigrette can be made a day ahead and refrigerated.

TIP: To section citrus fruit, cut off peel in strips, cutting deep enough to remove all of the white membrane and pith. Cut along both sides of each dividing membrane and remove sections.

PEPPERCORN IMPOSTOR

Pink peppercorns are not true peppercorns. Black, green and white peppercorns come from the *Piper nigrum* tree and are picked at different stages of ripeness, but the pink ones are the dried berries of the *Baies* rose plant. Although expensive, these pungent, almost sweet berries are worth seeking out at gourmet shops and Italian delis for their beautiful colour and unique flavour. They're sold dried or packed in brine or water.

Per serving:

342 calories, 34 g protein, 20.4 g fat, 4.4 g carbohydrate. Excellent source of vitamins B6, B12, thiamin, riboflavin and niacin. Excellent source of phosphorus.

Tangy Baked Salmon Fillets

Makes 4 servings

Simplicity often wins the day. This recipe is as straightforward as they come, but the result is superb. Because salmon can be assertive, here it's topped with just a few equally assertive elements: lemon zest, sun-dried tomatoes, garlic, parsley. Serve with fluffy couscous or rice, and a mild green vegetable such as steamed green beans or bok choy.

3	tablespoons (45 mL) chopped fresh Italian (flat-leaf) parsley
2	tablespoons (30 mL) grated lemon zest
2	tablespoons (30 mL) finely chopped, drained sun-dried tomatoes (packed in oil)
1	large garlic clove, minced
2	tablespoons (30 mL) olive oil
¼	teaspoon (1 mL) salt
¼	teaspoon (1 mL) pepper
4	salmon fillets (skin on), about 6 ounces (170 g) each

In small bowl, combine parsley, lemon zest, sun-dried tomatoes and garlic. Stir in oil, salt and pepper.

Place salmon fillets, skin side down, in greased baking dish large enough to hold fish in a single layer. Spread parsley mixture evenly over top of each fillet.

Bake at 450 F (230 C) for 10 minutes per inch (2.5 cm) of thickness or until fish flakes easily when tested with a fork. ○

ITALIAN (FLAT-LEAF) PARSLEY

For a stronger, more pronounced peppery taste and aroma, seek out fresh Italian (flat-leaf) parsley, rather than the milder curly leaf variety.

A FRESH SPIN ON PARSLEY

Thoroughly wash parsley to remove traces of grit. Though some cooks suggest washing herbs just before using them, we use parsley so frequently for both flavour and garnish in our test kitchen that it makes sense to wash it as soon as it's unloaded from the grocery bag. Loosen the bunch and rinse with tepid water. Then dry it thoroughly in a salad spinner (small salad spinners, slightly larger than a hefty cantaloupe, are perfect for this kind of job), or blot it dry using paper towel. Keep it in the fridge, stored one of two ways: Wrap in paper towel and place inside a plastic bag, then keep in crisper for up to 1 week. Or treat like a vase of flowers: Trim a little off the stems, then plunk the parsley in a glass partly filled with water, and tent loosely with a plastic bag. (For best results, change the water every few days.)

Per serving:
319 calories, 34.3 g protein, 18.4 g fat, 2.6 g carbohydrate. Excellent source of vitamins B6, B12, thiamin, riboflavin and niacin. Excellent source of phosphorus.

Salmon Steaks with Mango-Hazelnut Chutney

Makes 4 servings

HAZELNUT OR FILBERT?

What's the difference between a hazelnut and a filbert? They're two names for the same thing. Filbert, it is said by some, is derived from "full beard," because on some varieties the husk entirely covers the nut. Others say the name was adopted because in England, St. Philbert's day falls on August 22, and that's when the earliest nuts ripen. Commercial growers in British Columbia prefer to use "hazelnut," from the German haselnuss.

TIPS

• Hazelnuts have a slightly bitter dark brown skin — simply remove the skin by placing toasted nuts in a clean tea towel and rub until most of the skin is removed.

• To cook pappadams, lightly brush both sides with vegetable oil and enclose each one in paper towel. Microwave, one at a time, on High for 45 seconds or until puffy, turning over halfway through cooking time.

Per serving:

380 calories, 35.3 g protein, 20.4 g fat, 12.8 g carbohydrate. Excellent source of vitamins B6, B12, thiamin, riboflavin and niacin. Excellent source of magnesium and phosphorus.

This sauce is a study in balance: The potent flavours of mango chutney and mustard are smoothed and quieted by the light sour cream. Fresh mango, added to the chutney and nestled next to the salmon, draws the dish together. Basmati rice goes well with this dish, as do store-bought pappadams (a wafer-thin Indian bread) — just pop 'em in the microwave oven, and they swell and blister.

2	tablespoons (30 mL) hazelnuts
½	cup (125 mL) light sour cream
2	tablespoons (30 mL) mango chutney
1	teaspoon (5 mL) dijon mustard
1	tablespoon (15 mL) finely chopped shallot
	Salt and pepper
¼	cup (50 mL) finely diced mango
4	salmon steaks, about 6 ounces (170 g) each
	Vegetable oil
	Mango slices for garnish

Place hazelnuts on rimmed baking sheet and bake at 350 F (180 C) for 8 minutes or until fragrant. Remove nuts from oven and preheat broiler. Rub nuts in clean tea towel to remove skins; chop fine.

Meanwhile, combine sour cream, chutney, mustard, shallot, ¼ teaspoon (1 mL) salt and pinch pepper in small bowl. Stir in diced mango and toasted nuts; set aside.

Brush salmon steaks with oil. Lightly sprinkle with salt and pepper; place on greased broiler pan. Broil for 10 minutes per inch (2.5 cm) of thickness or until fish flakes easily when tested with a fork, turning once. Transfer to serving platter and garnish with mango slices. Serve with sour cream mixture. ⟳

Moroccan Salmon Steaks with Chermoula

Makes 4 servings

Just the name "chermoula" evokes the lush, resonant flavours of Moroccan cuisine. This vibrant, jade-green sauce is quintessentially Moroccan. You'll be tempted to make enough to have some left over for ... well, whatever you might cook the next day. (It could even be tucked into an omelette for breakfast.) Take a cue from Morocco's famous hospitality and serve this as a company dish, along with couscous spiked with chopped dried fruit.

Chermoula

¼	cup (50 mL) chopped fresh cilantro
¼	cup (50 mL) chopped fresh Italian (flat-leaf) parsley
1	small shallot, chopped coarse
1	garlic clove, chopped coarse
½	teaspoon (2 mL) ground cumin
⅛	teaspoon (0.5 mL) paprika
⅛	teaspoon (0.5 mL) salt
	Pinch cayenne pepper
1½	tablespoons (22 mL) lemon juice
1½	tablespoons (22 mL) olive oil

Salmon

4	salmon steaks, about 6 ounces (170 g) each
	Salt and pepper
	Lemon wedges

Chermoula: Place cilantro, parsley, shallot, garlic, cumin, paprika, salt and cayenne pepper in small food processor; pulse until very finely chopped. With motor running, add lemon juice and oil; process until combined.

Salmon: Lightly sprinkle salmon steaks with salt and pepper. Place steaks in lightly greased baking dish large enough to hold fish in a single layer. Spread top of each steak with 1 tablespoon (15 mL) chermoula.

Bake at 450 F (230 C) for 10 minutes per inch (2.5 cm) of thickness or until fish flakes easily when tested with a fork. Transfer to serving platter. Serve with lemon wedges. ⟲

To Roast Cumin

To maximize the flavour of cumin, roast seeds before grinding. Buying ground cumin may save time, but for superior flavour, start with whole seeds and roast them yourself: Use a small, dry heavy frypan over medium-high heat; add seeds and roast for 1 to 2 minutes or until fragrant and just slightly darkened, shaking pan constantly. Grind seeds in a mortar and pestle, or in a clean coffee grinder or spice grinder. Store ground cumin in clean spice jar away from heat and direct light.

Per serving:

295 calories, 34 g protein, 15.8 g fat, 2.2 g carbohydrate. Excellent source of vitamins B6, B12, thiamin, riboflavin and niacin. Excellent source of phosphorus.

D-Y-O (Design Your Own) Salmon Burgers

Makes 4 servings

Burgers are perennial favourites, and there's always room for a new take on the theme. If you've avoided making salmon patties because you don't like the flavour and texture canned salmon delivers, try using fresh fish. Rich, fresh salmon can give burgers the respect they deserve. When it comes to the fixin's, be your own designer — what will it be? A slice of red onion? Fresh dill? Onion marmalade? Aioli? Cream cheese? Arugula? Watercress? Iceberg lettuce? Pickles? Go to it.

1	pound (500 g) skinless salmon fillet
1	large egg
1	small jalapeno pepper, seeded and chopped fine
1	green onion, chopped fine
1	small garlic clove, minced
1	tablespoon (15 mL) finely chopped sweet pickled ginger
¾	teaspoon (4 mL) salt
¼	teaspoon (1 mL) pepper
¾	cup (175 mL) fresh bread crumbs
1	teaspoon (5 mL) vegetable oil

Remove and discard any bones in salmon fillet. Cut fillet into about 1-inch (2.5 cm) pieces and place in food processor; pulse until coarsely chopped.

In large bowl, lightly beat egg. Add jalapeno pepper, green onion, garlic, ginger, salt and pepper. Add salmon and bread crumbs; stir to mix. Shape mixture into 4 patties, about ½-inch (1 cm) thick (patties will be soft).

In large, heavy nonstick frypan, heat oil over medium heat. Add salmon burgers and cook for 8 minutes or until done, turning once. ⏱

Salmon Fillet Panini with Mesclun Greens

Makes 4 servings

Sometimes there's nothing more comforting than a delicious sandwich — taking big bitefuls, no knife or fork or spoon between you and pleasure. If you want a salmon sandwich and you want it sumptuous, then grill a fillet, just to moist flaky doneness, and not a moment longer. To conclude the meal, serve seasonal berries or sliced fruit with vanilla yogurt or sweetened whipped cream.

4	(6-inch/15 cm long) french rolls or hoagie buns
¼	cup (50 mL) olive oil
2	tablespoons (30 mL) lemon juice
2	garlic cloves, minced
4	thin skinless salmon fillets, about 4 ounces (125 g) each
	Salt and pepper
4	tablespoons (60 mL) dijonnaise
2	cups (500 mL) mesclun greens

Cut each roll in half lengthwise; place, cut side up, on baking sheet. Broil for 2 minutes or until golden; keep warm.

In small bowl, whisk together oil, lemon juice and garlic. Lightly sprinkle salmon fillets with salt and pepper; place on greased broiler pan. Brush with half the oil mixture. Broil for 10 minutes per inch (2.5 cm) of thickness or until fish flakes easily when tested with a fork, turning once and brushing with remaining oil mixture.

For each sandwich: Spread 1 tablespoon (15 mL) dijonnaise on bottom half of each roll; place 1 fillet on top, then add ½ cup (125 mL) mesclun greens and remaining bread half. ⏲

WHAT IS MESCLUN?

Mesclun (pronounced mehz-clan) is a mixture of young small salad greens (hence it's other name, "spring mix") that's sold both packaged and in bulk. The term means "mix" in the dialect of Nice, and it's deliberately vague. Mesclun always contains several types of salad leaves, and varies with the season and locale (arugula, dandelion, frisee, mache, oak leaf, radicchio and baby spinach appear often). The one constant is a pleasant jumble of shapes, colours, textures and flavours. To save time, purchase packaged, washed, ready-to-use mesclun.

TIP: Dijonnaise is a handy, creamy blend of mustard and mayonnaise found in the condiment section of supermarkets. If you don't have it, stir ½ teaspoon (2 mL) dijon mustard (or to taste) into 1 tablespoon (15 mL) mayonnaise.

Per serving:
338 calories, 13.3 g protein, 14.6 g fat, 38.7 g carbohydrate. Excellent source of vitamin B12, niacin and folate.

Teriyaki Salmon and Asparagus Stir-Fry

Makes 4 servings

SUBSTITUTION: You can use ¼ cup (50 mL) plus 3 tablespoons (45 mL) bottled teriyaki sauce in place of the soy sauce and mirin. Dozens of teriyaki sauces are available; we used San-J brand, which is delicately flavoured and thinner than some others. If you select a thicker sauce, you may have to dilute it with a little water.

Per serving:
235 calories, 27.6 g protein, 11.3 g fat, 7 g carbohydrate. Excellent source of vitamins B6, B12, C, thiamin, riboflavin, niacin and folate. Excellent source of phosphorus.

If you lead a busy life, then the trusty stir-fry is a reliable standby. A good stir-fry can be as quick to prepare as convenience food if the ingredients are kept to a minimum. In this one, asparagus and bell pepper provide the crunch, and salmon provides richness. Four ingredients are all it takes for the sauce. Serve atop Chinese egg noodles, tossed with sesame oil and soy sauce.

1	**pound (500 g) skinless salmon fillet**
	Salt and pepper
1	**tablespoon (15 mL) vegetable oil**
1	**pound (500 g) asparagus, trimmed and cut into 1½-inch (4 cm) pieces**
1	**yellow bell pepper, cut into thin strips**
¼	**cup (50 mL) soy sauce**
3	**tablespoons (45 mL) mirin (sweet Japanese rice wine)**
1	**teaspoon (5 mL) grated fresh ginger**
1	**tablespoon (15 mL) lime juice**
3	**green onions, sliced thin on the diagonal**
	Lime wedges

Pat salmon dry with paper towel. Cut into 1-inch (2.5 cm) pieces. Lightly sprinkle with salt and pepper. In large nonstick wok or heavy frypan, heat oil over medium-high heat. Add salmon to wok and stir-fry for 5 to 7 minutes or until fish flakes easily when tested with a fork, turning pieces very gently (if the salmon's surface starts to brown too quickly, lower the heat a little). With slotted spoon, transfer salmon to bowl and set aside.

Add asparagus to wok and stir-fry for 2 minutes. Add yellow pepper and stir-fry for 2 minutes or until vegetables are just tender-crisp; transfer to bowl with salmon. Add soy sauce, mirin, ginger and ¼ teaspoon (1 mL) pepper to wok; cook for 1 minute or until syrupy. Return salmon and vegetables to wok; cook for 1 minute or until heated through. Transfer to serving platter. Drizzle with lime juice and sprinkle green onions on top. Garnish with lime wedges. ☺

Creamy Pasta with Salmon and Shiitake Mushrooms

Makes 4 servings

Do you give wide berth to cream pastas, thinking they will park themselves around your waist? You can, of course, just have microscopic portions, but what's the fun in that? This pasta dish tastes perilously like cream sauce, only it's made with yogurt and chicken stock.

6	cups (1.5 L) broad noodles (about ¾ pound/350 g)
2	tablespoons (30 mL) butter, divided
1	pound (500 g) skinless sockeye salmon fillet (about ½-inch/1 cm thick), cut crosswise in half
	Salt and pepper
1	tablespoon (15 mL) vegetable oil
1	small onion, chopped
2	garlic cloves, minced
2	cups (500 mL) sliced, stemmed shiitake mushrooms (about ¼ pound/125 g)
1	tablespoon (15 mL) all-purpose flour
1	cup (250 mL) chicken stock
2	teaspoons (10 mL) lemon juice
1	cup (250 mL) thick plain yogurt (10 per cent M.F.)
3	tablespoons (45 mL) chopped fresh dill, divided

Cook noodles in large pot of boiling salted water until tender; drain and return to pot. Add 1 tablespoon (15 mL) butter and toss.

Meanwhile, sprinkle salmon pieces lightly with salt and pepper. In large heavy frypan, heat oil over medium-high heat. Add salmon and cook for 5 minutes or until fish flakes easily when tested with a fork, turning once. Transfer salmon to plate and keep warm. Remove any excess brown bits from bottom of pan and discard.

Add remaining 1 tablespoon (15 mL) butter to frypan and place over medium heat. Add onion and garlic; saute for 1 minute. Add mushrooms and saute for 3 minutes or until tender. Sprinkle with flour, ½ teaspoon (2 mL) salt and ¼ teaspoon (1 mL) pepper; stir to mix. Stir in stock and lemon juice; cook for 1 minute, stirring and scraping browned bits from bottom of pan. Remove frypan from heat and stir in yogurt and 2 tablespoons (30 mL) dill.

Cut salmon into bite-sized pieces; gently stir into sauce. Reduce heat to medium-low; return pan to stovetop until salmon and sauce are heated through, stirring frequently. Transfer noodles to serving platter; top with sauce. Sprinkle with remaining dill. ◑

WHAT ARE BROAD NOODLES?

Broad noodles are a good choice to serve as a nest beneath this creamy sauce, but any pasta you have on hand will do. Broad noodles made with whole eggs or yolks are richer and softer than plain wide wheat noodles. They are less likely to become overcooked and soggy.

WHAT IS THICK PLAIN YOGURT?

This product may take a little searching, but thick plain yogurt is well worth the hunt. At 10 per cent milk fat (that's the "M.F." number on the container), it pays off in recipes by adding luxurious texture to cooked sauces. Refrain from substituting a low-fat plain yogurt, as the resulting dish will taste slightly sour and the texture of the sauce will be thin and grainy. Light sour cream can be substituted but it doesn't have quite the same creamy texture and fresh flavour as the thick yogurt.

We had fine success using the Quebec-made brand called Liberty Mediterranée, which is sold in some supermarkets and at specialty cheese and dairy shops.

Per serving:
741 calories, 42.2 g protein, 30 g fat, 74.5 g carbohydrate. Excellent source of vitamins B6, B12, thiamin, riboflavin and niacin. Excellent source of magnesium, phosphorus and zinc.

Thai Green Curry with Salmon

Makes 4 servings

Though he claims to be a "heat coward," Vancouver Sun food writer Murray McMillan loves this mildly spicy dish, which he perfected for a story on curry diversity. We appreciate its virtues, too. McMillan included the recipe in The New Canadian Basics Cookbook *(published by Penguin), which he wrote with Carol Ferguson. Substitute prawns for the salmon, if you wish, or use a combination, he says. Serve in large bowls atop aromatic Thai jasmine rice — there's lots of sauce to go around. Adjust the amount of curry paste to suit your own level of bravery.*

1	(400 mL) can coconut milk, stirred and divided
¼	cup (50 mL) finely chopped shallots
1	teaspoon (5 mL) minced garlic
1	teaspoon (5 mL) finely chopped fresh ginger
2	teaspoons (10 mL) Thai green curry paste or to taste
2	tablespoons (30 mL) fish sauce or to taste
1	tablespoon (15 mL) lime juice, or 2 kaffir lime leaves, torn into thirds (see note)
1	pound (500 g) skinless salmon fillet, cut into bite-size pieces
1	cup (250 mL) snow peas, cut in half on the diagonal, or ½ cup (125 mL) frozen green peas
2	tablespoons (30 mL) chopped fresh basil
2	tablespoons (30 mL) chopped fresh cilantro
	Salt and pepper

In large frypan over medium-high heat, bring ½ cup (125 mL) coconut milk to a boil. Add shallots, garlic and ginger; cook for 2 minutes, stirring constantly. Add green curry paste and cook for 1 minute or until dissolved, stirring constantly. Add remaining coconut milk, fish sauce and lime juice; boil gently for 2 minutes or until slightly thickened.

Add salmon; reduce heat and simmer for 2 minutes, stirring occasionally. Add snow peas and simmer for 3 minutes or until fish flakes easily when tested with a fork. Stir in basil and cilantro. Add salt and pepper to taste. ↺

Note: If using kaffir lime leaves, remove and discard after cooking — they're chewy and inedible unless sliced very finely.

WHAT ARE KAFFIR LIME LEAVES?

The kaffir lime tree produces fruit similar to the common lime, but with a much more textured, almost knobbly skin. The limes' zest as well as the leaves impart a pungent lemony-lime flavour. Fresh kaffir leaves are available in Asian markets and can be frozen for later use.

WHAT IS FISH SAUCE?

This amber liquid is made from salted, fermented fish, and it's readily identifiable by its pungent aroma, which dissipates when cooked. The thin sauce, also known as nam pla, is widely used in Southeast Asia, and is indispensible for many Thai and Vietnamese dishes.

WHAT IS THAI GREEN CURRY PASTE?

It's a balanced, flavourful blend of numerous ingredients, which can include coriander root, galangal, garlic, lemon grass, kaffir lime leaves, fresh green chilies and shrimp paste. Hotter than red curry paste, it's traditionally used in coconut-based curry sauces.

Per serving:
390 calories, 28.1 g protein, 28.4 g fat, 7.6 g carbohydrate. Excellent source of vitamins B6, B12, thiamin, riboflavin, niacin and folate. Excellent source of iron, magnesium and phosphorus.

Crispy Cornmeal and Parmesan Cod

Makes 4 servings

This crisp golden coating adds eye appeal to that old reliable, cod. (Sometimes pieces of cod just look too, too plain.) Break through the coating and you find fish that is flaky and succulent. Complete the plate with parslied nugget potatoes, tossed in a little butter, and a bright green vegetable such as spinach or broccoli.

½	**cup (125 mL) grated parmesan cheese**
¼	**cup (50 mL) cornmeal**
1	**large garlic clove, minced**
½	**teaspoon (2 mL) salt**
⅛	**teaspoon (0.5 mL) pepper**
½	**teaspoon (2 mL) dried oregano leaves**
½	**cup (125 mL) plain yogurt**
2	**tablespoons (30 mL) milk**
4	**cod fillets, about 6 ounces (170 g) each**

In pie plate or shallow dish, combine parmesan cheese, cornmeal, garlic, salt, pepper and oregano. In small bowl, combine yogurt and milk.

Dip cod fillets in yogurt mixture, then coat with parmesan mixture. Place on greased broiler pan and broil for 10 minutes per inch (2.5 cm) of thickness or until fish flakes easily when tested with a fork. ⏱

TIP: Be sure to use freshly grated parmesan cheese, preferably from a block of good Parmigiano-Reggiano. Grating takes only an extra minute or two, but the difference in flavour and texture is more than worth the time. If you opt to buy already grated parmesan, pick up a plastic tub or resealable bag of cheese from the grocer's dairy cooler. Avoid the granular parmesan that stands at room temperature on supermarket shelves — it's bland, and as enticing as sawdust.

Per serving:

214 calories, 30.4 g protein, 5.5 g fat, 8.8 g carbohydrate. Excellent source of vitamins B6, B12 and niacin. Excellent source of calcium and phosphorus.

Fish Nuggets with Dipping Sauce

Makes 4 servings

Kids can develop a hankering for cod when it's presented as fun to eat, the way it is here — small chunks served with whatever dipping sauce you know will appeal to them. Cornflakes and parmesan encase the fish and add flavour as well as structure. Serve this with home-made coleslaw, or if you're really pressed for time, buy the slaw ready-made at a favourite deli.

2	tablespoons (30 mL) light mayonnaise
2	tablespoons (30 mL) plain yogurt
1	teaspoon (5 mL) lemon juice
1	garlic clove, minced
1	green onion, chopped fine
⅓	cup (75 mL) cornflake crumbs
2	tablespoons (30 mL) grated parmesan cheese
1	teaspoon (5 mL) paprika
¼	teaspoon (1 mL) salt
⅛	teaspoon (0.5 mL) cayenne pepper
1	pound (500 g) cod fillets, cut into 1½-inch (4 cm) pieces
	Mild salsa or other favourite dipping sauce

In small bowl, combine mayonnaise, yogurt, lemon juice, garlic and green onion. In pie plate or shallow dish, combine cornflake crumbs, parmesan cheese, paprika, salt and cayenne pepper; set aside.

Dip cod pieces in mayonnaise mixture, then coat with crumb mixture. Place on greased baking sheet. Bake at 450 F (230 C) for 8 minutes or until fish flakes easily when tested with a fork. Serve with salsa. ⏲

PICK A BONE

To ensure complete removal of bones from fish fillets, lay fillet flat on work surface and gently rub your fingers over the entire flesh surface; if you detect a bone, remove it with tweezers.

Per serving:
172 calories, 24.7 g protein, 3.8 g fat, 8.5 g carbohydrate. Excellent source of vitamins B6, B12 and niacin.

Pine Nut Cod Burgers

Makes 4 servings

Sturdy cod gets a flavour boost from pine nuts and parmesan in these pleasing burgers. But there's a surprise element as you take your first bite: A mix of yogurt, lime and basil adds bright, light notes. Freshly squeezed lime juice is essential. Any large, crusty (preferably chewy) rustic bun will work for this fish burger. You want something large enough to hold the fish fillet, and that has a texture that won't become soggy quickly. Check neighbourhood bakeries for interesting options — sourdough, herb-flecked, whole-grain, sun-dried tomato or olive studded; the variety is endless. Pick up roasted root vegetables from the deli or make your own.

⅓   **cup (75 mL) finely chopped pine nuts**
4   **tablespoons (60 mL) grated parmesan cheese**
4   **thin cod fillets, about 4 ounces (125 g) each**
    Salt and pepper
    Olive oil
½   **cup (125 mL) thick plain yogurt (10 per cent M.F.)**
1   **teaspoon (5 mL) lime juice**
1   **tablespoon (15 mL) finely chopped fresh basil**
4   **Portuguese or other large buns, split**
4   **tomato slices**
    Lettuce

In pie plate or shallow dish, combine pine nuts and parmesan cheese. Lightly sprinkle cod fillets with salt and pepper; brush both sides lightly with oil. Coat evenly with pine nut mixture, pressing lightly into fish.

Place cod in baking pan large enough to hold fish in single layer. Bake at 450 F (230 C) for 10 minutes per inch (2.5 cm) of thickness or until fish flakes easily when tested with a fork. Remove from oven and keep warm. Preheat broiler.

While fish is baking, combine yogurt, lime juice and basil in small bowl. Add salt and pepper to taste.

Place buns under broiler for 2 minutes or until lightly toasted.

For each burger: Spread bun with 2 tablespoons (30 mL) yogurt mixture. Put 1 piece of fish in bun; top with 1 tomato slice and lettuce. ↻

QUICK-ROASTED VEGETABLES

1½   **pounds (750 g) root vegetables (carrots, parsnips, potatoes, sweet potatoes or turnips)**
2   **tablespoons (30 mL) olive oil**
1   **tablespoon (15 mL) finely chopped fresh herb (oregano, rosemary, sage or thyme)**
    Salt and pepper

Peel and cut vegetables into slices just under ¼-inch (5 mm) thick; pat dry with paper towels. In large bowl, combine oil, herb and ½ teaspoon (2 mL) salt; add vegetables and toss to coat. With slotted spoon, remove vegetables from bowl and place in single layer on greased rimmed baking sheet.

Roast at 450 F (230 C) for 18 to 20 minutes or until tender on the inside and crisp on the outside, turning vegetables once half-way through roasting time.

Sprinkle with salt and pepper to taste.

Makes 4 servings.

Per burger:
297 calories, 16.5 g protein, 13.8 g fat, 28.8 g carbohydrate.

Hoisin-Glazed Snapper

Makes 4 servings

Anyone who's enjoyed the richness of hoisin sauce in something like mu shu pork knows what a powerful flavour addition it can be. (The sauce is a mixture of soy beans, garlic, sugar, spices and salt.) This recipe takes the volume up a notch by adding other Asian staples: soy sauce, sesame oil and the heat of chili paste. Suddenly snapper gains a whole new persona. Steamed green beans or broccoli, plus steamed rice, make fitting accompaniments.

2	tablespoons (30 mL) hoisin sauce
1	tablespoon (15 mL) soy sauce
1	teaspoon (5 mL) sesame oil
¼	teaspoon (1 mL) hot chili paste
2	tablespoons (30 mL) finely chopped green onion, divided
4	snapper fillets, about 6 ounces (170 g) each
	Salt and pepper
2	tablespoons (30 mL) chopped fresh cilantro

In small bowl, combine hoisin sauce, soy sauce, sesame oil, chili paste and 1 tablespoon (15 mL) chopped green onion.

Lightly sprinkle snapper fillets with salt and pepper; place on greased broiler pan. Brush top of fillets with half the hoisin sauce mixture. Broil for 10 minutes per inch (2.5 cm) of thickness or until fish flakes easily when tested with a fork, turning once and brushing with remaining hoisin sauce mixture.

Transfer fillets to serving platter. Sprinkle with cilantro and remaining 1 tablespoon (15 mL) green onion.

Per serving:
202 calories, 35.5 g protein, 3.5 g fat, 5 g carbohydrate. Excellent source of vitamins B6, B12 and niacin. Excellent source of magnesium and phosphorus.

Grilled Halibut with Black Bean Sauce

Makes 4 servings

If you like a little sass with your seafood, black bean garlic sauce, jazzed up with lime juice (fresh, please) and grated ginger will give it some kick and meld with the delicately smoky barbecued flavour of halibut. Try it with stir-fried baby bok choy and steamed rice.

2	tablespoons (30 mL) black bean garlic sauce
1	tablespoon (15 mL) lime juice
1	teaspoon (5 mL) vegetable oil
1	teaspoon (5 mL) finely grated fresh ginger
4	(1-inch/2.5 cm thick) halibut fillets, about 6 ounces (170 g) each
	Salt and pepper
1	green onion, chopped fine
	Fresh cilantro leaves

In small bowl, combine black bean garlic sauce, lime juice, oil and ginger; spread lightly over both sides of halibut fillets.

Place fillets on greased barbecue grill over medium-high heat and cook for 10 minutes per inch (2.5 cm) of thickness or until fish flakes easily when tested with a fork, turning once.

Transfer fillets to serving platter. Season to taste with salt and pepper. Sprinkle with green onion and garnish with cilantro. ○

WHAT IS BLACK BEAN GARLIC SAUCE?

Black bean garlic sauce is a seasoning used in many Asian cuisines. It's made with mashed fermented soy beans, garlic and occasionally star anise, and while rather thin in consistency, it packs intense flavour — a little goes a long way. Readily found in Asian stores and the oriental section of most supermarkets. Once opened, store the jar in the refrigerator. If purchasing a can of this sauce, make sure you transfer any unused sauce to a non-metal container and refrigerate for up to 6 months.

Per serving:
208 calories, 36 g protein, 5.2 g fat, 1.9 g carbohydrate. Excellent source of vitamins B6, B12 and niacin. Excellent source of magnesium and phosphorus.

Broiled Halibut with Fresh Tarragon Butter

Makes 4 servings

TARRAGON TIME

Tarragon's sophisticated flavour is an essential in French cuisine. It's distinctive — use sparingly until you know how much you like. Always look for French tarragon — its narrow green leaves offer a bitter-sweet, peppery taste with anise undertones. Russian tarragon, on the other hand, can be bitter and more pungent.

Sometimes the best meals are the simplest — especially when the focal point is fresh fish. Halibut doesn't need a lot of adornment — it can dazzle the palate almost alone. But add a contrasting flavour, whether sweet, salty or tart, and you have a winner. Here the faintly licorice charm of tarragon goes perfectly with this meaty fish. Should you have a little extra time, go beyond the usual rice or potato accompaniment and try a grain dish such as a millet, quinoa or barley pilaf.

2	tablespoons (30 mL) butter, at room temperature
2	teaspoons (10 mL) chopped fresh parsley
2	teaspoons (10 mL) finely chopped fresh tarragon
1	teaspoon (5 mL) lemon juice
	Salt and pepper
2	tablespoons (30 mL) olive oil
1	tablespoon (15 mL) lemon juice
1	garlic clove, minced
4	halibut steaks, about 6 ounces (170 g) each

In small bowl, combine butter, parsley, tarragon, 1 teaspoon (5 mL) lemon juice, and pinch each of salt and pepper; mix well. Set aside.

In another small bowl, whisk together oil, 1 tablespoon (15 mL) lemon juice and garlic. Lightly sprinkle halibut steaks with salt and pepper; place on greased broiler pan. Brush with half the oil mixture. Broil for 10 minutes per inch (2.5 cm) of thickness or until fish flakes easily with a fork, turning once and brushing with remaining oil mixture. Top each steak with an equal portion of butter mixture. ○

Per serving:
300 calories, 35.5 g protein, 16.6 g fat, 0.4 g carbohydrate. Excellent source of vitamins B6, B12 and niacin. Excellent source of magnesium and phosphorus.

Halibut Steaks with Lemon Butter

Makes 4 servings

Lemon and seafood make a classic combination for good reason. Lemon is the perfect foil for the delicate richness of many types of fish. In this recipe, the lemon plays a prominent role in a compound butter: lemon zest and green onion mixed with room-temperature butter. If you like to eat a lot of fish, compound butters made with herbs and other seasonings take only a few minutes to prepare and are excellent enhancements.

4   **(1-inch/2.5 cm thick) halibut steaks, about 6 ounces (170 g) each**
     Salt and pepper
1   **tablespoon (15 mL) vegetable oil**
2   **tablespoons (30 mL) butter, at room temperature**
½   **teaspoon (2 mL) finely grated lemon zest**
2   **teaspoons (10 mL) finely chopped green onion**
     Chopped green onion for garnish
4   **lemon wedges**

Preheat oven to 450 F (230 C).

Lightly sprinkle halibut steaks with salt and pepper. In large cast-iron or other heavy ovenproof frypan, heat oil over medium-high heat. Add steaks and cook on 1 side for 3 minutes or until browned. Turn steaks over and place frypan in oven. Bake for 5 to 7 minutes or until fish flakes easily when tested with a fork.

Meanwhile, combine butter, lemon zest and 2 teaspoons (10 mL) green onion in small bowl.

Top each steak with an equal amount of butter mixture. Garnish with green onion and serve with a lemon wedge. ◔

TIP: For a fine frozen asset, make extra herb butter and shape in log-like rolls; wrap completely in plastic wrap and place in freezer bag. When ready to use, slice off just what you need and let come to room temperature.

Per serving:
272 calories, 35.6 g protein, 13.2 g fat, 1.5 g carbohydrate. Excellent source of vitamin B12 and niacin. Excellent source of magnesium and phosphorus.

Grilled Halibut Steaks with Sun-Dried Tomato Pesto

Makes 4 servings

Traditional pesto is a classic from Genoa that's made with basil, garlic, pine nuts, parmesan and olive oil. Used loosely, the term describes a thick, paste-like sauce, and that's the idea behind sun-dried tomato pesto. When combined with butter, parsley and lime juice, it does a fine job of complementing halibut cooked on the outdoor grill. When fresh corn is in season, serve a cob alongside the fish, plus sliced field tomatoes with a sprinkle of snipped fresh chives.

2	tablespoons (30 mL) butter, at room temperature
1	teaspoon (5 mL) sun-dried tomato pesto
1	tablespoon (15 mL) chopped fresh parsley
1½	teaspoons (7 mL) lime juice
4	halibut steaks, about 6 ounces (170 g) each
	Vegetable oil
	Salt and pepper
	Lime wedges

In small bowl, combine butter, pesto, parsley and lime juice; set aside.

Lightly brush halibut steaks with oil. Lightly sprinkle with salt and pepper. Place steaks on greased barbecue grill over medium-high heat and cook for 10 minutes per inch (2.5 cm) of thickness or until fish flakes easily when tested with a fork, turning once. Transfer steaks to serving platter. Top each steak with about 2 teaspoons (10 mL) butter mixture. Serve with lime wedges. ○

HOW THICK SHOULD FISH STEAKS OR FILLETS BE?

For best results when grilling or broiling, they should be no thicker than 1 inch (2.5 cm). That lets you cook the inside before the outside starts to overcook and dry out.

PICK YOUR PESTO

Besides the classic basil pesto, many other versions are now available. Their intense flavours are well worth exploring. Sun-dried tomato pesto comes both in jars and in sealed plastic pouches that are usually in the refrigerated fresh pasta section of supermarkets.

TIP: Fish steaks are crosscut through the body of the fish. You pay for bones and skin, but they help keep the fish together during grilling.

Per serving:
262 calories, 35.6 g protein, 12.2 g fat, 0.3 g carbohydrate. Excellent source of vitamins B6, B12 and niacin. Excellent source of magnesium and phosphorus.

Steamed Manila Clams with Gazpacho Vinaigrette
Makes 4 servings

You'll love this dish in late summer, when tomatoes are lush and full of flavour, and you're looking for a cooling supper. This recipe, created by Karen Barnaby, chef at The Fish House in Stanley Park in Vancouver, received five stars from our taste panel. It's a meal-in-a-bowl, layered with gazpacho, clams and garlic bruschetta (which sponges up the last morsels of flavour). Dig in. Then move on to a refreshing finish of watermelon or other juicy summer melons for dessert.

Gazpacho vinaigrette

1	pound (500 g) tomatoes, chopped (about 2 large)
½	red bell pepper, chopped coarse
½	English cucumber, peeled, seeded and chopped
1	garlic clove, minced
3	tablespoons (45 mL) red wine vinegar
1	tablespoon (15 mL) olive oil
½	cup (125 mL) cold water
1	teaspoon (5 mL) granulated sugar
½	teaspoon (2 mL) salt
	Cayenne pepper
2	tablespoons (30 mL) finely chopped onion
1	tablespoon (15 mL) finely chopped fresh cilantro

Steamed clams

4	(½-inch/1 cm thick) slices Italian bread
1	garlic clove
	Olive oil
2	pounds (1 kg) fresh manila clams (in shell)
	Fresh cilantro sprigs

Gazpacho vinaigrette: Put tomatoes, bell pepper, cucumber, garlic, vinegar, oil, water, sugar, salt and cayenne pepper to taste in food processor. Pulse until vegetables are almost pureed, scraping down sides of bowl. Taste and adjust seasoning by adding more salt, sugar and red wine vinegar, if necessary. Stir in onion and chopped cilantro.

(continued on following page)

MAKE AHEAD: The gazpacho vinaigrette can be prepared (without the onion and cilantro), covered and refrigerated for up to 2 days. Remove from refrigerator and let come to room temperature before proceeding with recipe. Add onion and chopped cilantro just before serving.

Per serving:
247 calories, 12.3 g protein, 9.4 g fat, 29.5 g carbohydrate. Excellent source of vitamins B12, C and folate. Excellent source of iron.

TIP: Search out reputable fish markets and supermarkets that have a rapid turnover of fresh seafood. Once you get your clams home, place in large bowl, cover with damp tea towel and refrigerate, then use as soon as possible — within 1 day. Fresh clams are best cooked the day they're bought.

Steamed clams: Broil or grill both sides of the bread for 1 to 2 minutes or until golden. Rub with garlic clove and drizzle with oil; set aside.

Scrub clams thoroughly; rinse and drain. Put clams with 2 tablespoons (30 mL) water in heavy pot with tight fitting lid. Turn heat to high and steam clams for 2 to 3 minutes or until shells open. Discard any clams that do not open.

Spoon about ¾ cup (175 mL) vinaigrette into each of 4 large soup bowls, reserving about ½ cup (125 mL) for garnish. Place 1 slice of the garlic-rubbed bread on top of vinaigrette in each bowl. Divide clams and some of their juice among the bowls. Drizzle reserved vinaigrette over top and garnish with cilantro sprigs. Serve immediately. ○

Sizzling Prawns
Makes 4 servings

Prawns are exceptionally versatile — they're good almost any way you serve them, except overcooked. Plump, succulent prawns don't need a lot of embellishment to make them stars of the grill, but a few carefully chosen flavours amplify the seafood's appeal. Here, they are speared on skewers and sizzled on the barbecue. Try serving these prawns atop noodles that have been tossed with butter and chopped fresh chervil.

2	tablespoons (30 mL) purchased olive oil flavoured with hot peppers
2	tablespoons (30 mL) lime juice
2	tablespoons (30 mL) finely chopped fresh basil
1	tablespoon (15 mL) grated fresh ginger
2	garlic cloves, crushed
24	deveined peeled raw prawns (about ¾ pound/350 g)
	Salt and pepper

In small bowl, whisk together oil and lime juice; stir in basil, ginger and garlic.

Put prawns in medium bowl. Add 2 tablespoons (30 mL) oil-lime mixture and stir to coat prawns; reserve remaining oil-lime mixture. Let prawns marinate for 15 minutes.

Remove prawns from marinade and thread on to metal skewers. Place on greased barbecue grill over medium-high heat; cook for 3 to 5 minutes or until pink, turning once and basting twice with reserved oil-lime mixture. Sprinkle with salt and pepper to taste. ↻

HOT OIL

For this prawn recipe, we used Consorzio brand Roasted Red Pepper Olive Oil with chilies, which is pleasantly mild when first tasted, but like a wave will eventually unfurl a hidden heat intensity. Many hot pepper oils are available in specialty stores, Asian markets and some supermarkets — they vary considerably in their heat levels. Whichever you choose, do some testing beforehand and adjust the quantity to ensure the oil won't overpower the prawns.

Per serving:
142 calories, 15.3 g protein, 8.2 g fat, 1.4 g carbohydrate. Excellent source of vitamin B12.

East-Meets-West Scallop Spaghettini

Makes 4 servings

When you pat scallops dry just before they hit a hot frypan, they sear, and gain a deliciously crisp outer surface, rather than braise in their own juices. Timing is crucial — you don't want their satiny texture to turn chewy and stringy.

While waiting for the pasta water to boil, rinse scallops and assemble all the other ingredients. Start cooking the sauce after the spaghettini goes into the boiling water — dinner will be ready in under 10 minutes. This lightly seasoned dish is easy enough for a weeknight supper and elegant enough for entertaining. Serve with a coleslaw made using napa cabbage, julienned carrots and red bell pepper.

¾	**pound (350 g) spaghettini**
1	**pound (500 g) bay scallops**
¼	**cup (50 mL) chicken stock**
2	**tablespoons (30 mL) dry sherry**
1	**tablespoon (15 mL) soy sauce**
¾	**teaspoon (4 mL) sesame oil**
2	**tablespoons (30 mL) vegetable oil**
2	**garlic cloves, minced**
2	**teaspoons (10 mL) finely chopped fresh ginger**
2	**green onions, chopped fine**
	Salt and pepper
4	**tablespoons (60 mL) chopped fresh cilantro, divided**

Cook spaghettini in large pot of boiling salted water until tender; drain and return to pot.

Meanwhile, rinse scallops; drain and pat dry with paper towels.

In small bowl, combine stock, sherry, soy sauce and sesame oil; set aside.

In large heavy frypan, heat vegetable oil over medium-high heat. Add garlic, ginger, green onions and scallops; saute for 3 minutes or until opaque. Add salt and pepper to taste. With slotted spoon, transfer scallops to bowl; set aside.

Add stock mixture to scallop liquid in frypan; increase heat to high and cook for 2 to 3 minutes or until liquid is slightly thickened. Return scallops to frypan and heat through. Stir in 3 tablespoons (45 mL) of the cilantro. Add to pasta in pot; toss. Transfer to serving platter. Sprinkle with remaining 1 tablespoon (15 mL) cilantro. ⏲

TIP: For convenience, keep a good supply of frozen bay scallops (about the size of large grapes) in the freezer. They're sold in bulk in supermarkets — 1 pound (500 g) frozen scallops is about 4 cups (1 L). The night before you plan to serve this dish remove scallops from freezer; place in bowl, cover, and let thaw in refrigerator. If you can't find the small bay scallops, use larger scallops and cut into quarters.

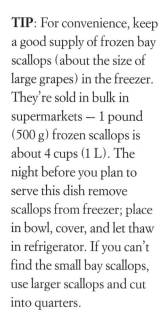

Per serving:
516 calories, 32.3 g protein, 10.2 g fat, 69.1 g carbohydrate. Excellent source of vitamin B12 and niacin. Excellent source of magnesium, phosphorus and zinc.

Rotini with Tuna, Grape Tomatoes and Black Olives

Makes 4 servings

As always, the better the ingredients, the more likely your dish is to please. So if it's within your budget and time frame, please use the parmesan you actually grate, not the kind you shake out of a container. You'll be further rewarded if you use olives with some intensity, from an Italian or Greek deli (forget the watery canned kind).

4	cups (1 L) rotini
3	tablespoons (45 mL) olive oil
1	onion, chopped fine
2	garlic cloves, minced
¼	teaspoon (1 mL) dried crushed hot red pepper
2	(170 g) cans solid white tuna (packed in water), drained and separated into small chunks
2	cups (500 mL) grape or cherry tomatoes, halved
⅓	cup (75 mL) slivered pitted black olives
½	cup (125 mL) chopped fresh Italian (flat-leaf) parsley Salt and pepper
¼	cup (50 mL) grated parmesan cheese

Cook rotini in large pot of boiling salted water until tender; drain, reserving ½ cup (125 mL) pasta water. Set reserved pasta water aside. Return pasta to pot.

Meanwhile, heat oil in large heavy frypan over medium-high heat. Add onion, garlic and dried red pepper; saute for 3 minutes. Stir in tuna, tomatoes and olives; cook for 2 minutes or until heated through. Stir in reserved pasta water.

Add tuna mixture to pasta and toss. Add parsley, and salt and pepper to taste. Transfer to serving platter. Sprinkle with parmesan cheese. ⟳

MINI-TOMATOES

Grape tomatoes look like baby plum tomatoes. If you can't find them, use cherry tomatoes. In a pinch, a couple of regular hothouse or field tomatoes can be seeded and coarsely chopped.

TIME SAVER: If possible, buy pitted black olives in brine. We used kalamata olives — dark brine-cured Greek olives, each slit to increase flavour penetration. We find most canned olives are a waste of money — they're too mild, and the texture can be mushy.

Per serving:
601 calories, 36.7 g protein, 17.9 g fat, 71.9 g carbohydrate. Excellent source of vitamins B6, B12 and niacin. Excellent source of iron, magnesium and phosphorus.

Hurry Up Tortiglioni with Salmon and Pine Nuts

Makes 4 servings

When imagination and cupboards stand all but empty, there's always canned salmon, around which you can pull together an entirely satisfying meal. If you have capers and sun-dried tomatoes in the fridge and lots of pasta, it's a matter of making sure you have pine nuts and some vegetables to add. For a salad, mix chunks of cucumber and tomatoes with big handfuls of herbal greens, such as Italian (flat-leaf) parsley, watercress, cilantro or arugula.

4	cups (1 L) tortiglioni pasta (large spiral-edged tubes)
3	tablespoons (45 mL) pine nuts
3	tablespoons (45 mL) olive oil from bottled sun-dried tomatoes
1	onion, chopped
1	red bell pepper, diced
1	cup (250 mL) sliced mushrooms (about 3 ounces/85 g)
2	tablespoons (30 mL) chopped, drained sun-dried tomatoes (packed in oil)
2	tablespoons (30 mL) drained capers
2	(213 g) cans sockeye salmon, drained and separated into small chunks
	Salt and pepper
¼	cup (50 mL) grated parmesan cheese

Cook tortiglioni in large pot of boiling salted water until tender; drain and return to pot.

Meanwhile, toast pine nuts in dry, large heavy frypan over medium heat for 3 to 5 minutes or until golden, stirring and shaking pan frequently. Remove from pan and set aside.

In same frypan, heat oil over medium-high heat. Add onion, red pepper and mushrooms; saute for 5 minutes or until vegetables are tender-crisp. Stir in pine nuts, sun-dried tomatoes and capers.

Add mushroom mixture and salmon to pasta; toss. Add salt and pepper to taste. Transfer to serving platter. Sprinkle with parmesan cheese. ☾

SUBSTITUTION: Use your favourite curly pasta such as rotini or fusilli to stand in for the tortiglioni. Whichever short, stubby pasta you choose, make sure it has texture so that it will capture the sauce.

Per serving:

694 calories, 34.7 g protein, 28.9 g fat, 74.2 g carbohydrate. Excellent source of vitamins A, B12, C, niacin and folate. Excellent source of calcium, iron, zinc, magnesium and phosphorus. High in fibre.

Can-Do Tuna-Soy Rotini

Makes 4 servings

Dinner's in the can — or three cans, to be exact — when you opt for this sunny pasta dish. All you need to have on hand is some stubby pasta and canned tuna, stewed tomatoes and soy beans. Using Italian-style stewed tomatoes means most of the seasoning is already done for you. For a bright salad alongside, place slices of melon and cucumbers atop a bed of spicy greens, such as watercress or arugula.

3	cups (750 mL) rotini
1	tablespoon (15 mL) olive oil
1	small onion, chopped
1	(398 mL) can Italian-style stewed tomatoes
⅓	cup (75 mL) chopped fresh parsley
¼	teaspoon (1 mL) dried crushed hot red pepper or to taste
¼	teaspoon (1 mL) salt
¼	teaspoon (1 mL) pepper
1	(398 mL) can black soy beans, drained and rinsed
1	(170 g) can solid white tuna (packed in water), drained and separated into small chunks
2	teaspoons (10 mL) lemon juice
⅓	cup (75 mL) grated parmesan cheese

Cook rotini in large pot of boiling salted water until tender; drain.

Meanwhile, heat oil in large heavy saucepan over medium-high heat. Add onion and saute for 3 minutes or until tender. Add tomatoes, parsley, dried red pepper, salt and pepper; cook for 1 minute, stirring occasionally. Stir in beans and tuna; cook for 1 minute. Stir in lemon juice.

Put pasta on serving platter and top with tomato mixture. Sprinkle with parmesan cheese. ⏲

TIP: We prefer canned solid white tuna over chunk or flaked tuna; its firm texture and appearance are superior. Use a fork to separate solid tuna into pieces; you'll be impressed by how well it holds its shape in salads and pastas.

Per serving:
516 calories, 31.9 g protein, 14.4 g fat, 66.1 g carbohydrate. Excellent source of vitamin B12, niacin and folate. Excellent source of iron, magnesium and phosphorus. High in fibre.

Prawn and Pesto Pizza

Makes 4 to 6 servings

PRAWNS OR SHRIMP?

These shellfish are delicious, but casual use of the terms on packages of frozen imported products and in seafood stores leads to confusion. Shrimp and prawns are part of one big family — the difference lies in size. "Prawn" once denoted the larger clan members, and shrimp were, well, shrimps — little guys. Because bigger is equated with better in the marketplace, what were once called "medium" or "large" shrimp may now be sold as small prawns. Keep in mind both the number you need for the recipe, and what that number should weigh. Use it as a guide to the quantity and size you need, however they're labelled.

TIP: Light provolone cheese is sold sliced and packaged in supermarket deli sections. Lay slices on top of one another in order to grate.

You'll wonder why you ever bothered dialling for pizza delivery when you find you can make this family-pleaser in less than 30 minutes. The blend of pesto, mild cheeses and prawns is a winning partnership. Serve with a crisp green salad with thinly sliced fennel and red or yellow bell peppers.

4	tablespoons (60 mL) basil pesto
2	(12-inch/30 cm) purchased, prebaked thin pizza crusts
2	cups (500 mL) grated light provolone cheese
1/4	cup (50 mL) unripened soft goat cheese, cut into small pieces
4	tablespoons (60 mL) slivered, drained sun-dried tomatoes (packed in oil)
36	cooked, shelled small prawns (about 1/2 pound/250 g)
4	tablespoons (60 mL) thinly sliced green onions
	Coarsely ground pepper
4	to 6 lemon wedges

For each pizza: Spread half the pesto evenly over pizza crust, leaving 1/2-inch (1 cm) border all around. Sprinkle with half the provolone cheese. Top with half the goat cheese and sun-dried tomatoes. Arrange half the prawns evenly over top.

Bake at 450 F (230 C) for 10 minutes or until cheese is melted and toppings are hot.

Sprinkle with half the green onions. Sprinkle with pepper to taste. Serve with lemon wedges. ⏱

Per serving:
926 calories, 45.4 g protein, 27.1 g fat, 124 g carbohydrate. Excellent source of vitamin B12, thiamin, riboflavin and niacin. Excellent source of calcium, iron, zinc and phosphorus. Very high in fibre.

Extravagant Crab-Smothered Pizza

Makes 4 to 6 servings

If you want to serve the ultimate luxury pizza, here it is. Crab, melted cheese and just a hint of jalapeno make this a special-occasion treat. Serve with crudites and a store-bought dip, such as hummus or roasted red pepper.

½	pound (250 g) cooked fresh crabmeat
4	teaspoons (20 mL) olive oil
2	(12-inch/30 cm) purchased, prebaked thin pizza crusts
1½	cups (375 mL) grated part-skim mozzarella cheese
2	large jalapeno peppers, seeded and chopped fine
2	shallots, chopped fine
½	cup (125 mL) grated asiago cheese
2	teaspoons (10 mL) butter
4	teaspoons (20 mL) lemon juice
1	large plum tomato, chopped fine
2	tablespoons (30 mL) chopped green onion
	Salt and pepper
4	to 6 lemon wedges

Using fork, shred crabmeat.

For each pizza: Brush 2 teaspoons (10 mL) olive oil evenly over pizza crust, leaving ½-inch (1 cm) border all around. Sprinkle with ¾ cup (175 mL) mozzarella cheese. Top with half the jalapeno peppers and shallots. Sprinkle with ¼ cup (50 mL) asiago cheese. Bake at 450 F (230 C) for 10 to 12 minutes or until cheese is melted.

Melt butter in microwave; stir in lemon juice. Top pizza with half the crabmeat and drizzle with half the butter mixture. Sprinkle with half the tomato and 1 tablespoon (15 mL) green onion. Sprinkle with salt and pepper to taste. Serve with lemon wedges. ○

GREAT FOR ENTERTAINING

TIP: Asiago is a sharp-tasting cow's milk cheese with a rich nutty flavour. It's sold both in blocks and already grated. In a pinch, old white cheddar cheese could be substituted.

SUBSTITUTION: Use fresh crabmeat whenever possible, but if desperation hits, substitute 2 (170 g) cans crabmeat (drain well). Note that some canned crabmeat is high in sodium, so adjust any added salt according to taste.

Per serving:
870 calories, 40.7 g protein, 24.8 g fat, 119.6 g carbohydrate. Excellent source of vitamin B12, thiamin, riboflavin, niacin and folate. Excellent source of calcium, iron, zinc, magnesium and phosphorus. High in fibre.

CHAPTER FOUR

Vegetarian

To get the best results,
you should
talk to your vegetables.

Prince Charles

Lentil Soup with Fresh Vegetables

Makes 4 servings

Tiny but powerful, lentils deliver plenty of protein, carbohydrates, folic acid, iron and potassium. This soup, with sun-dried tomato pesto, carrots, cauliflower and spinach, can be made in a jiffy using canned lentils. If you'd prefer more cauliflower and less spinach, go ahead and adjust the recipe to your liking. For a more substantial meal, serve the soup with quickly grilled cheese quesadillas or toasted multigrain bread.

1	**tablespoon (15 mL) olive oil**
1	**onion, chopped**
2	**large garlic cloves, minced**
½	**cup (125 mL) thinly sliced carrots**
1	**tablespoon (15 mL) sun-dried tomato pesto**
4	**cups (1 L) vegetable stock**
1	**cup (250 mL) small cauliflower florets**
¼	**teaspoon (1 mL) dried thyme leaves**
4	**cups (1 L) lightly packed fresh spinach, chopped coarse**
1	**(540 mL) can lentils, drained and rinsed**
1	**tablespoon (15 mL) lemon juice**
	Salt and pepper

In large heavy saucepan, heat oil over medium-high heat. Add onion, garlic and carrots; saute for 3 minutes or until onion is tender. Remove from heat and stir in pesto until well mixed with vegetables. Add stock, cauliflower and thyme. Place over high heat and bring to a boil. Reduce heat and simmer for 3 minutes or until cauliflower and carrots are almost tender. Stir in spinach and lentils; heat through, about 2 minutes. Remove from heat and stir in lemon juice. Add salt and pepper to taste.

TIME SAVER: Buy washed, ready-to-use spinach: A 283 gram package yields about 12 cups (3 L) lightly packed.

TIP: Classic pesto is made of basil, garlic, pine nuts, parmesan cheese and olive oil, but pesto is now available in many other flavours. We used bottled sun-dried tomato pesto; similar pesto is sold packaged and refrigerated in the fresh pasta section of some supermarkets.

Per serving:

179 calories, 9.5 g protein, 5.6 g fat, 25.1 g carbohydrate. Excellent source of vitamins A, C and folate. Excellent source of iron and magnesium. Very high in fibre.

TIME SAVER: For optimum flavour use fresh vegetable stock; otherwise, reconstituted vegetable stock cubes will suffice.

White Bean and Vegetable Soup

Makes 6 servings

The beauty of this particularly easy soup is that it doesn't require any sauteing. Simply combine all the readily available ingredients in one big pot, and heat. Dig into your freezer and pull out any combination of mixed vegetables. We used a package that contained green beans, carrots, corn and peas. To keep this a gentle soup, be careful with the hot pepper sauce — unless, of course, you like a lot of heat. Accompany the soup with wedges of hefty sourdough or Irish soda bread.

2	(398 mL) cans Italian-style stewed tomatoes
6	cups (1.5 L) vegetable stock
2	(398 mL) cans navy beans, drained and rinsed
3	cups (750 mL) frozen mixed vegetables
½	cup (125 mL) chopped fresh parsley
	Dash hot pepper sauce
	Salt and pepper
6	tablespoons (90 mL) grated parmesan cheese

In large saucepan, combine stewed tomatoes, stock and beans. Bring to a boil over high heat. Add frozen vegetables and return to a boil; reduce heat and simmer for 2 minutes. Add parsley, hot pepper sauce, and salt and pepper to taste.

Sprinkle each serving with 1 tablespoon (15 mL) parmesan cheese. ◔

Per serving:

245 calories, 14.7 g protein, 3.1 g fat, 44 g carbohydrate. Excellent source of vitamins A, C, thiamin and folate. Excellent source of iron and magnesium. Very high in fibre.

Greek Pasta Salad

Makes 4 servings

Why mess with a good thing, you might ask. Think of this as a value-added salad. Take what makes a Greek salad tick (tomatoes, cucumber, feta cheese, kalamata olives) and add pasta and kidney beans — it's especially good for hot weather dining. Just add a loaf of crusty bread to complete the meal.

3	cups (750 mL) small shell pasta
1	(398 mL) can red kidney beans, drained and rinsed
2	tomatoes, chopped coarse
2	cups (500 mL) cubed English cucumber
⅓	cup (75 mL) thinly sliced red onion
¾	cup (175 mL) crumbled feta cheese
½	cup (125 mL) pitted kalamata olives
⅓	cup (75 mL) shredded fresh basil
½	cup (125 mL) Greek-style dressing (purchased or home-made)
	Salt and pepper

Cook pasta in large pot of boiling salted water until tender. Drain and rinse pasta with cold water; drain well. Place in large bowl. Add beans, tomatoes, cucumber, onion, feta cheese, olives and basil to pasta.

Drizzle salad with dressing and toss. Add salt and pepper to taste. Transfer to serving platter. ↻

Note: Several brands of shell pasta are labelled "small size shells." Don't use the very small type that are usually added to soups, or the large size that can be stuffed — pick a medium size.

MEDITERRANEAN DRESSING

⅓	cup (75 mL) olive oil
2	tablespoons (30 mL) red wine vinegar
1	teaspoon (5 mL) dijon mustard
1	garlic clove, minced
¼	teaspoon (1 mL) salt
¼	teaspoon (1 mL) pepper
	Pinch dried oregano

In small bowl, whisk together all ingredients. Makes about ½ cup (125 mL).

TIME SAVER: Pitted kalamata olives can be hard to find, so when you locate a good source, make a note of it. (Best bets are Greek and Italian markets.) Pitting whole olives for this salad only takes about 5 minutes, but the cook might prefer a 5-minute breather in the kitchen.

Per serving:

883 calories, 28.2 g protein, 30.6 g fat, 126 g carbohydrate. Excellent source of vitamin B6, thiamin, riboflavin and niacin. Excellent source of iron, zinc, magnesium and phosphorus. Very high in fibre.

Warm Potato Salad with Dark Greens

Makes 4 servings

WHAT IS ARUGULA?

Also known as rocket, arugula resembles smooth, elongated oak leaves. The bright green leaves are sold in bunches and have a distinct mild peppery flavour. If you can't find arugula, substitute curly endive, spinach or watercress.

SUBSTITUTION: We think the knobbly little nugget potatoes (with their wisps of skin still attached) that come to market in the late spring and early summer are the best tasting, but any small new potato could be used. For an eye-catching salad try a combination of small new red, purple and white potatoes.

Per serving:

386 calories, 8.4 g protein, 16.2 g fat, 56.6 g carbohydrate. Excellent source of vitamins A, B6, C, niacin and folate. Excellent source of magnesium and phosphorus. Very high in fibre.

Classic cold potato salads make great picnic fare, but warm potato salads are much more sophisticated. Here's a version in which the flavours are amplified by sun-dried tomatoes, red onion and olives. Be sure to mix the dressing with the potatoes while they're still warm, so they soak up the flavours. For a tempting presentation, nestle the potato salad in a ring of crisp dark greens. (Peppery arugula makes a delicious contrast.) To round out the meal, just add another salad of sliced bocconcini and tomatoes, drizzled with extra-virgin olive oil and sprinkled with finely chopped fresh basil. Be sure to alert family and friends about the unpitted olives in the salad.

2½	**pounds (1.125 kg) nugget potatoes (unpeeled)**
1	**fennel bulb**
¼	**cup (50 mL) extra-virgin olive oil**
¼	**cup (50 mL) lemon juice**
2	**teaspoons (10 mL) finely chopped, drained sun-dried tomatoes (packed in oil)**
1	**teaspoon (5 mL) grainy mustard (with seeds)**
1	**teaspoon (5 mL) liquid honey**
¼	**cup (50 mL) finely chopped red onion**
1	**red bell pepper, julienned**
16	**nicoise olives**
½	**cup (125 mL) finely chopped fresh Italian (flat-leaf) parsley, divided**
	Salt and pepper
1	**bunch arugula or spinach**

Cook potatoes in large pot of boiling water for 15 minutes or until tender; drain.

While potatoes cook, cut fennel bulb in half lengthwise, then cut each half crosswise into thin slices. In large bowl, whisk together oil, lemon juice, sun-dried tomatoes, mustard and honey. Stir in fennel, onion, red pepper, olives and half the parsley. Add potatoes while they're still hot; mix well. Add salt and pepper to taste.

Arrange arugula around outside edge of large serving platter and pile potato mixture in the middle. Sprinkle with remaining parsley. ⟳

Vegetable Fusilli and Black Bean Salad

Makes 4 to 6 servings

When the mercury's rising, you want meals that are cooling, and if they're portable for picnics, so much the better. This pasta salad lends itself to an al fresco experience. Dry fusilli (little pasta twists) in vegetable flavours is readily available in supermarkets, as are canned black beans, but you can substitute other kinds of beans. The choice of cheese is flexible, too: Swiss or mozzarella would work; for something more refined, use goat cheese or brie. Pack some carrot sticks, celery and hard-cooked eggs to complete the feast.

3	cups (750 mL) vegetable fusilli pasta
1	(398 mL) can black beans, drained and rinsed
4	green onions, sliced
2	tomatoes, seeded and chopped coarse
1	small red bell pepper, sliced thin
1/3	cup (75 mL) chopped fresh basil
1/4	pound (125 g) part-skim mozzarella or swiss cheese, julienned
1	cup (250 mL) vinaigrette (purchased or home-made)
	Salt and pepper
	Fresh basil leaves, optional

Cook fusilli in large pot of boiling salted water until tender. Drain and rinse pasta with cold water; drain well.

In large bowl, combine beans, green onions, tomatoes, red pepper, chopped basil, mozzarella cheese and pasta. Add vinaigrette and toss. Add salt and pepper to taste. Transfer to large serving platter and garnish with basil leaves. ○

BALSAMIC VINAIGRETTE

1/2	cup (125 mL) olive oil
1/4	cup (50 mL) white balsamic vinegar
3	tablespoons (45 mL) lemon juice
3/4	teaspoon (4 mL) salt
1/2	teaspoon (2 mL) pepper
1/2	teaspoon (2 mL) dijon mustard
3	garlic cloves, minced
1	large shallot, chopped fine

In small bowl, whisk together all ingredients. Makes about 1 cup (250 mL).

TIP: Probably the most expensive of the onion clan, tender shallots are best known for their mild, complex flavour. They look like a large garlic bulb and can have two or three segmented cloves. In our recipes, one shallot refers to the whole bulb not just one clove.

Per serving:

709 calories, 24.7 g protein, 35.1 g fat and 75.8 g carbohydrate. Excellent source of vitamins A, C, thiamin, riboflavin, niacin and folate. Excellent source of iron, zinc, magnesium and phosphorus. Very high in fibre.

Tomato, Artichoke and Feta Couscous Salad

Makes 4 servings

TIME SAVER: Feta cheese can be purchased already crumbled in packages or plastic tubs in the dairy or produce sections of supermarkets. Feta varies in saltiness — be sure to taste the salad before adding more salt.

Per serving:

698 calories, 20.5 g protein, 38.5 g fat, 69.8 g carbohydrate. Excellent source of niacin and folate. Excellent source of calcium, magnesium and phosphorus. High in fibre.

Couscous is a secret weapon for combatting dinner prep stress. Just add boiling water (or stock), wait for it to be absorbed and that's it. In North Africa, couscous is the traditional base for hearty stews, but we've taken this granular pasta and run in another direction by adding salad ingredients and dressing. For a side dish, pick up a container of hummus and serve it with carrot sticks and slices of whole-wheat baguette.

Couscous

1¾ cups (425 mL) water

¼ teaspoon (1 mL) salt

2 tablespoons (30 mL) lemon juice

1½ cups (375 mL) couscous

Salad

1 cup (250 mL) grape or cherry tomatoes, quartered

1 cup (250 mL) crumbled light feta cheese

½ cup (125 mL) thinly sliced red onion

⅓ cup (75 mL) pitted kalamata olives, halved

1 (170 mL) jar marinated artichoke hearts, drained and halved

4 tablespoons (60 mL) chopped fresh parsley, divided

⅔ cup (150 mL) herb vinaigrette (purchased or home-made)

Salt and pepper

Couscous: In large saucepan, combine water and salt; cover and bring to a boil. Stir in lemon juice. Stir in couscous; cover and remove from heat. Let stand for 5 minutes. Transfer couscous to large bowl and fluff with fork; let cool for about 15 minutes, fluffing with fork frequently.

Salad: Add tomatoes, feta cheese, onion, olives, artichokes and 2 tablespoons (30 mL) parsley to couscous; stir to mix. Add vinaigrette and toss to mix. Add salt and pepper to taste. Transfer to serving platter. Sprinkle with remaining 2 tablespoons (30 mL) parsley. ⟳

Curried Couscous with Dried Apricots and Lentils

Makes 4 servings

Here's an example of globetrotting cooking. We took directional signals from India, North Africa and North America to create a spicy grain-based dish with tiny explosions of apricot. To accompany this couscous, buy some Indian flatbread — naan or chapatis.

Sour cream sauce

1	cup (250 mL) light sour cream
2	tablespoons (30 mL) lemon juice
2	green onions, chopped
	Salt and pepper

Couscous

2	tablespoons (30 mL) vegetable oil, divided
1	onion, chopped (divided)
1¾	cups (425 mL) vegetable stock
¼	cup (50 mL) slivered dried apricots
1½	cups (375 mL) couscous
3	garlic cloves, minced
1	teaspoon (5 mL) curry powder
½	teaspoon (2 mL) ground cumin
1	red bell pepper, sliced thin
1	(540 mL) can lentils, drained and rinsed
8	cups (2 L) lightly packed fresh spinach, chopped coarse

Sour cream sauce: In small bowl, combine sour cream, lemon juice and green onions. Add salt and pepper to taste; set aside.

Couscous: In large heavy saucepan, heat 1 tablespoon (15 mL) oil over medium-high heat. Add half the onion and saute for 3 minutes. Add stock, cover and bring to a boil. Stir in apricots and couscous. Cover and remove from heat. Let stand for 5 minutes. Fluff with fork and cover.

Meanwhile, heat remaining 1 tablespoon (15 mL) oil in large heavy frypan over medium heat. Add remaining onion and garlic; saute for 2 minutes. Add curry powder and cumin; saute for 1 minute. Add red pepper and saute for 2 minutes or until vegetables are tender-crisp. Add lentils and heat through, stirring constantly. Add spinach and stir until it just starts to wilt. Remove from heat.

Fluff couscous again; add to vegetable mixture and stir to mix. Add salt and pepper to taste. Transfer to serving platter. Serve with sour cream sauce. ○

WHAT IS COUSCOUS?

Couscous on its own is one of the world's great convenience foods — ready to eat in just 5 minutes.

It is the smallest of all pastas, granular in texture and made from semolina (ground durum wheat) that is mixed with water and made into tiny pellets. (Semolina refers to the type of grind — fine but not powdery.) When used as the basis for a major dish, it becomes a culinary tradition of some North African countries — Morocco, Algeria and Tunisia, where it's cooked in a couscoussiere. The semolina is steamed in the upper part of the pot while a spicy stew simmers in a layer below.

TIME SAVER: Purchase washed, ready-to-use spinach: A 283 gram package yields about 12 cups (3 L) lightly packed.

TIP: To warm naan, stack and wrap bread in damp cloth. Microwave on High for 30 to 40 seconds or until warm.

Per serving:

557 calories, 24.2 g protein, 12.3 g fat, 89.6 g carbohydrate. Excellent source of vitamins A, B6, C, thiamin, riboflavin, niacin and folate. Excellent source of iron, zinc, magnesium and phosphorus. Very high in fibre.

Couscous with Currants, Peppers and Squash

Makes 4 servings

Currants and couscous partner well, and not just for their alliteration. Currants give the little pebbles of pasta sweetness, and complement the chickpeas and butternut squash, as well. Toss in chopped jalapeno for a little vibrant heat, and this becomes a lively main course.

1	cup (250 mL) light sour cream
3	tablespoons (45 mL) lime juice, divided
4	tablespoons (60 mL) chopped fresh basil, divided
	Salt and pepper
1¾	cups (425 mL) vegetable stock
⅓	cup (75 mL) currants
1½	cups (375 mL) couscous
2	tablespoons (30 mL) olive oil
1	onion, chopped
1	jalapeno pepper, seeded and chopped fine
1	garlic clove, minced
¼	pound (125 g) piece butternut squash, peeled and cut into ¼-inch (5 mm) dice
1	red bell pepper, cut into thin strips
1	cup (250 mL) sliced mushrooms (about 3 ounces/85 g)
1	cup (250 mL) drained, canned chickpeas, rinsed

In small bowl, combine sour cream, 2 tablespoons (30 mL) lime juice and 2 tablespoons (30 mL) basil. Add salt and pepper to taste; set aside.

Put stock in large saucepan; cover and bring to a boil. Stir in currants, remaining 2 tablespoons (30 mL) basil and 1 tablespoon (15 mL) lime juice. Stir in couscous; cover and remove from heat. Let stand for 5 minutes. Fluff with fork and cover.

Meanwhile, heat oil in large heavy frypan over medium heat. Add onion, jalapeno pepper, garlic and squash; saute for 3 minutes. Add red pepper and mushrooms; saute for 3 minutes or until vegetables are tender-crisp. Stir in chickpeas and heat through.

Fluff couscous again; add vegetables and stir to mix. Add salt and pepper to taste. Transfer to serving platter. Serve with sour cream sauce. ⟲

Per serving:

524 calories, 17.9 g protein, 13.1 g fat, 85 g carbohydrate. Excellent source of vitamins A, C, niacin and folate. Excellent source of iron, magnesium and phosphorus. High in fibre.

Polenta-Mushroom Stew

Makes 4 servings

Embellished with parmesan cheese, polenta is a delicious comfort food and a perfect match with the earthy flavours of mushrooms. Here we've used shiitake and button mushrooms to broaden this heavenly match. Grilled vegetables make a fine accompaniment to this dish. When shopping, check the package to make sure you're getting a quick-cooking polenta, one that's ready in about five minutes.

Polenta

3½	cups (875 mL) water
1	teaspoon (5 mL) salt
1	cup (250 mL) quick-cooking polenta
⅓	cup (75 mL) grated parmesan cheese

Stew

1	onion
2	tablespoons (30 mL) vegetable oil
2	garlic cloves, minced
3	cups (750 mL) thickly sliced button mushrooms (about ½ pound/250 g)
2	cups (500 mL) thickly sliced, stemmed shiitake mushrooms (about ¼ pound/125 g)
1	(398 mL) can tomatoes (undrained), chopped
2	tablespoons (30 mL) chopped, drained sun-dried tomatoes (packed in oil)
2	teaspoons (10 mL) dijon mustard
8	cups (2 L) lightly packed fresh spinach, chopped coarse
	Salt and pepper

Polenta: In large bowl, combine water and salt; microwave on High for 7 minutes or until boiling. Stir in polenta and microwave for 4½ minutes, whisking every 2 minutes. Stir in parmesan cheese.

Meanwhile, make stew: Cut onion in half lengthwise, then cut each half crosswise into thin slices. In large heavy frypan, heat oil over medium-high heat. Add onion and garlic; saute for 3 minutes or until tender. Add button and shiitake mushrooms; saute for 2 minutes or until just tender. Add canned tomatoes, sun-dried tomatoes and mustard; simmer for 2 minutes, stirring occasionally. Stir in spinach and cook for 1 minute. Add salt and pepper to taste. Serve over polenta. ↺

WHAT IS POLENTA?

Coarse cornmeal is a staple in northern Italy, where it is often cooked into a dish called polenta, which has the consistency of cream of wheat. It can be mixed with butter or parmesan cheese, and eaten hot; or cooled until firm and cut into slices, then fried. Serve creamy polenta as a side dish in place of mashed potatoes.

Look for boxes of quick-cooking polenta (instant cornmeal) in specialty stores — it can be ready in about 5 minutes whether you cook it in the microwave or on top of the stove. Just remember that you must stir it constantly if you choose stovetop cooking.

TIME SAVER: Use kitchen scissors to chop canned tomatoes right in the can. You'll save both prep time and cleanup.

Per serving:

260 calories, 10.7 g protein, 12.9 g fat, 30.2 g carbohydrate. Excellent source of vitamin B6, riboflavin, niacin and folate. Excellent source of magnesium. Very high in fibre.

TIPS

- The secret to the taste and texture of this vegetarian chili is a soy-based alternative to ground beef. We used the widely available Yves brand Veggie Ground Round, with fine results. Look for it in the refrigerated section of supermarket produce departments.

- For a spicier chili, increase hot pepper sauce, or add 1 large finely chopped jalapeno pepper to the vegetables when cooking.

Per serving:

228 calories, 15.4 g protein, 4.3 g fat, 35.7 g carbohydrate. Excellent source of vitamins B12, C, thiamin, niacin and folate. Excellent source of iron, zinc and magnesium. Very high in fibre.

Gotcha!
Black Bean Chili

Makes 4 servings

If you have a beef with meat, you'll like this chili. A fine soy product stands in for ground beef, and could fool an unsuspecting diner. Beginner vegetarians can enjoy it while easing into meatlessness, because this chili has the heft of traditional versions, without the meat. Our tasters were quite oblivious to the absence of meat, until told. Make this the centrepiece of a warm, comforting meal by adding a spinach and avocado salad, and a substantial loaf of bread — corn bread is great, if you can find it.

1	tablespoon (15 mL) vegetable oil
1	onion, chopped
¼	cup (50 mL) chopped celery
2	garlic cloves, minced
2	(398 mL) cans stewed tomatoes
1	bay leaf
1	tablespoon (15 mL) chili powder
¼	teaspoon (1 mL) dried oregano leaves
	Salt and pepper
¼	teaspoon (1 mL) chipotle or other hot pepper sauce
1	(398 mL) can black beans, drained and rinsed
⅓	(340 g) package Veggie Ground Round, crumbled (about ¾ cup/175 mL)

In large heavy saucepan, heat oil over medium-high heat. Add onion, celery and garlic; saute for 3 minutes or until vegetables are tender.

Add stewed tomatoes, bay leaf, chili powder, oregano, ¼ teaspoon (1 mL) salt and chipotle pepper sauce; bring to a boil. Cover, reduce heat and simmer for 8 minutes, stirring occasionally.

Stir in beans and Veggie Ground Round; cover and cook for 3 minutes or until heated through. Remove bay leaf and discard. Add salt and pepper to taste. ♂

Grown-Up Mac 'n' Cheese

Makes 6 servings

When you're hungering for the soothing simplicity of macaroni-and-cheese, resist the temptation to reach for that sterile, additive-laced box on the kitchen shelf. Making one-pot macaroni-and-cheese is almost as easy as opening that box, and the results are far superior (and cleanup is easy, too). The cheeses this recipe calls for are designed to appeal to an adult palate, but it's easy to make a kid-pleasing version by substituting cheddar for the provolone and asiago. Add vegetable goodness to this meal with a plate of crudités (cauliflower, red and yellow bell pepper slices, radishes, fennel) and a store-bought dip.

4	cups (1 L) elbow macaroni
1	cup (250 mL) milk (1 per cent M.F.)
3	large eggs
3½	cups (875 mL) finely grated provolone cheese
½	cup (125 mL) finely grated asiago cheese
2	tablespoons (30 mL) butter
	Salt and pepper
	Chopped fresh parsley

Cook macaroni in large pot of boiling salted water until tender; drain and return to pot.

Meanwhile, whisk together milk and eggs until thoroughly blended. Stir into hot pasta, then add provolone cheese, asiago cheese and butter; stir until well mixed. Place over medium-low heat and cook for 3 to 5 minutes or until cheese has melted and sauce is creamy, stirring constantly. Add salt and pepper to taste. Serve sprinkled with parsley. ⟳

SUBSTITUTION: Use 4 cups (1 L) grated cheese in total: 3 cups (750 mL) cheddar and 1 cup (250 mL) provolone.

Per serving:

637 calories, 33.4 g protein, 28.9 g fat, 59.2 g carbohydrate. Excellent source of vitamin B12, riboflavin and niacin. Excellent source of calcium, phosphorus and zinc.

Rotini with Roasted Vegetables and Fresh Sage

Makes 4 servings

Roasting vegetables brings out a sweet intensity that's hard to beat. Here roasted asparagus, tomatoes, bell pepper and onion are tossed with pasta, vegetable stock, goat cheese and sun-dried tomatoes. Each element retains its own identity. This dish has special appeal in spring, when abundant fresh asparagus is so tempting.

½	**pound (250 g) asparagus, trimmed and cut into 1-inch (2.5 cm) pieces**
2	**tomatoes, cut into chunks**
1	**red bell pepper, cut into 1-inch (2.5 cm) pieces**
½	**red onion, sliced thin**
4	**garlic cloves, halved**
2	**tablespoons (30 mL) olive oil**
1	**tablespoon (15 mL) chopped fresh sage**
	Salt and pepper
4	**cups (1 L) rotini**
¼	**cup (50 mL) hot vegetable stock**
¼	**cup (50 mL) unripened soft goat cheese**
1	**tablespoon (15 mL) chopped, drained sun-dried tomatoes (packed in oil)**
¼	**cup (50 mL) grated parmesan cheese**

In large bowl, combine asparagus, tomatoes, red pepper, onion and garlic. Combine oil, sage and ¼ teaspoon (1 mL) each of salt and pepper; add to vegetables and toss.

Place all of the vegetables except asparagus in single layer on large greased rimmed baking sheet. Roast at 450 F (230 C) for 10 minutes. Stir in asparagus and roast for another 5 to 7 minutes or until vegetables are tender.

Meanwhile, cook rotini in large pot of boiling salted water until tender; drain and return to pot. Add roasted vegetables and their juices, hot stock, goat cheese and sun-dried tomatoes; toss. Add salt and pepper to taste. Transfer to serving platter. Sprinkle with parmesan cheese.

Per serving:

627 calories, 23.3 g protein, 17.6 g fat, 94.6 g carbohydrate. Excellent source of vitamin C and calcium. Very high in fibre.

Radiatore with Beans and Spinach

Makes 4 servings

Radiatore is Italian for radiator — a wintery symbol, but any chill is soon banished by this warming dish. What dark January evening wouldn't be brightened by a bowl of pasta in which hearty kidney beans are complemented by the bright flavours of carrots, garlic, red pepper, spinach and lemon juice? But don't get hung up on the seasons. Make it in mid-August, too, and serve with fresh corn on the cob, and a garden fresh salad.

4	cups (1 L) radiatore
2	cups (500 mL) purchased, ready-to-use peeled mini carrots
2	tablespoons (30 mL) olive oil
1	small onion, chopped
2	garlic cloves, minced
1	large red bell pepper, cut into thin strips
1	(398 mL) can red kidney beans, drained and rinsed
8	cups (2 L) lightly packed fresh baby spinach
1	tablespoon (15 mL) lemon juice
	Salt and pepper
½	cup (125 mL) grated parmesan cheese

Cook radiatore in large pot of boiling salted water until tender, adding carrots during last 7 minutes of pasta cooking time; drain and return pasta and carrots to pot.

Meanwhile, heat oil in large pot over medium heat. Add onion and garlic; saute for 2 minutes. Add red pepper and saute for 2 minutes. Add beans and spinach; cook for 1 minute or until spinach is wilted, stirring frequently. Stir in lemon juice, pasta and carrots. Add salt and pepper to taste. Transfer to serving platter. Sprinkle with parmesan cheese. ♻

TIP: The playfully named radiatore (little radiator-shaped chunks with ruffled edges) are perfectly designed for capturing pasta sauce. Any well-textured small pasta could be used, such as rotelle, small shells, fusilli or rotini.

Per serving:

297 calories, 15 g protein, 11.9 g fat, 36.5 g carbohydrate. Excellent source of vitamins A, C and folate. Excellent source of magnesium and phosphorus. Very high in fibre.

Farfalle with Uncooked Tomato Sauce

Makes 4 servings

This recipe deserves a speeding ticket. Broccoli and cauliflower cook in the same pot as the pasta. Meanwhile, the uncooked sauce, a medley of fresh tomatoes, green onions, basil and chopped sun-dried tomatoes, is ready as fast as you can chop. Ripe flavourful tomatoes are a must for this garden-fresh pasta sauce. Make a refreshing salad of butter lettuce, chopped Italian (flat-leaf) parsley, thinly sliced bosc pears and walnuts.

2½	cups (625 mL) farfalle (medium-size bow pasta)
1½	cups (375 mL) small cauliflower florets
1½	cups (375 mL) small broccoli florets
1	pound (500 g) plum tomatoes, chopped fine (2½ cups/625 mL)
½	cup (125 mL) chopped green onions
1	teaspoon (5 mL) dried basil leaves
2	tablespoons (30 mL) vegetable oil
2	tablespoons (30 mL) chopped, drained sun-dried tomatoes (packed in oil)
1	garlic clove, minced
	Salt and pepper
¼	cup (50 mL) grated parmesan cheese

Cook farfalle in large pot of boiling salted water until tender, adding cauliflower for the last 3 minutes of pasta cooking time and broccoli for the last 2 minutes; drain and return pasta and vegetables to pot.

Meanwhile, combine tomatoes, green onions, basil, oil, sun-dried tomatoes and garlic in large bowl.

Add hot pasta and vegetables to tomato mixture; toss. Add salt and pepper to taste. Transfer to serving platter. Sprinkle with parmesan cheese.

TIP: Sun-dried tomatoes are available bottled in supermarkets or in small plastic tubs in some delis. The flavour varies, so experiment until you find one you like. They may seem expensive, but most recipes only use a small amount, and they add lots of flavour.

Per serving:

383 calories, 14.1 g protein, 10.7 g fat, 60.6 g carbohydrate. Excellent source of vitamin C and folate. Excellent source of magnesium. High in fibre.

Gnocchi Alfredo with Broccoli and Shiitake Mushrooms

Makes 4 servings

Need dinner on the table in less than 20 minutes? With a selection of dried pasta and commercial sauces in the pantry, and a few items in the fridge, it's surprisingly easy to accomplish.

This smooth, creamy dish is made with dried gnocchi pasta, not to be confused with fresh gnocchi. (Fresh gnocchi are thumb-sized dumplings made from potato and flour, often with additional flavours such as eggs, cheese and spinach.) The dried pasta version resembles small ripple-edged shells, and those ripples lap up the delicious sauce. Serve with a green salad that includes watercress, and garnish with grape tomatoes.

4	cups (1 L) dried gnocchi pasta
3	cups (750 mL) small broccoli florets
2	tablespoons (30 mL) olive oil
1	onion, chopped
2	garlic cloves, minced
2	cups (500 mL) thinly sliced, stemmed shiitake mushrooms (about ¼ pound/125 g)
1	teaspoon (5 mL) chopped fresh thyme
½	cup (125 mL) dry white wine
1	(435 mL) jar alfredo pasta sauce
	Salt and pepper
¼	cup (50 mL) grated asiago cheese
¼	cup (50 mL) chopped fresh Italian (flat-leaf) parsley

Cook gnocchi in large pot of boiling salted water until tender, adding broccoli during last 2 minutes of pasta cooking time; drain and return pasta and broccoli to pot.

Meanwhile, heat oil in large heavy frypan over medium-high heat. Add onion and garlic; saute for 3 minutes or until tender. Reduce heat to medium and add mushrooms and thyme; saute for 3 minutes or until tender. Add wine and cook for 30 seconds. Add pasta sauce and cook for 1 minute or until heated through.

Add sauce to pasta and broccoli; toss. Add salt and pepper to taste. Transfer to serving platter. Sprinkle with asiago cheese and parsley. ⏱

TIP: Alfredo sauces are sold in jars and refrigerated pouches. Experiment with the various flavours: classic, roasted garlic, sun-dried tomato.

Per serving:

703 calories, 20.6 g protein, 27.9 g fat, 88.9 g carbohydrate. Excellent source of vitamin C, niacin and folate. Excellent source of magnesium and zinc. High in fibre.

Rotini with Fresh Tomatoes, Black Beans and Feta

Makes 4 servings

TIME SAVER: Feta cheese can be purchased already crumbled in packages or plastic tubs. This cheese varies in saltiness — be sure to taste this pasta dish before adding more salt.

TIP: To seed a tomato, cut in half horizontally, then use a spoon to remove seeds and pulp. Alternatively, gently squeeze in one hand to remove seeds and pulp.

Black beans, feta and sun-dried tomatoes impart earthy, salty flavours to this dish, while the fresh tomato gives it a bright lift. Serve with a baby spinach salad, tossed with toasted pecans.

3	tomatoes, seeded and diced (about 2 cups/500 mL)
¼	cup (50 mL) chopped, drained sun-dried tomatoes (packed in oil)
2	tablespoons (30 mL) olive oil
1	large garlic clove, minced
	Salt and pepper
4	cups (1 L) rotini
1	(398 mL) can black beans, drained and rinsed
¼	cup (50 mL) finely shredded fresh basil
¼	cup (50 mL) chopped green onions
½	cup (125 mL) crumbled feta cheese

In large bowl, combine fresh tomatoes, sun-dried tomatoes, oil, garlic and ½ teaspoon (2 mL) each of salt and pepper; set aside.

Cook rotini in large pot of boiling salted water until tender; drain and return to pot. Add tomato mixture and toss. Add beans, basil and green onions; toss. Add salt and pepper to taste. Transfer to serving platter. Sprinkle with feta cheese. ○

SUBSTITUTION: Instead of rotini, use penne rigate (penne with ridged sides), fusilli or rotelle.

Per serving:

562 calories, 22 g protein, 13.8 g fat, 88.7 g carbohydrate. Excellent source of thiamin, riboflavin, niacin and folate. Excellent source of iron, zinc, magnesium and phosphorus. Very high in fibre.

Rotini with Swiss Chard and Pine Nuts

Makes 4 servings

Swiss chard is a member of the beet family that's grown for its pleasantly tart leaves; shredded, they mix well with pasta. Chard contains substantial amounts of vitamin A and potassium, and respectable amounts of vitamin C and fibre. In this recipe, pine nuts add richness and dried hot red pepper adds a lick of heat. Serve with toasted baguette slices, topped with purchased tapenade (a thick seasoned black olive spread), thin tomato slices and a sprinkle of grainy sea salt.

¾	pound (350 g) swiss chard (green), trimmed
3	cups (750 mL) rotini
2	tablespoons (30 mL) vegetable oil, divided
¼	cup (50 mL) pine nuts
1	tablespoon (15 mL) butter
1	onion, chopped
1	garlic clove, minced
	Pinch dried crushed hot red pepper
¼	cup (50 mL) vegetable stock
	Salt and pepper
½	cup (125 mL) grated parmesan cheese, divided

Remove stalks from chard and chop; set aside. Coarsely chop leaves. (You should have about 10 cups/2.5 L lightly packed leaves.)

Cook rotini in large pot of boiling salted water until tender; drain and return to pot. Add 1 tablespoon (15 mL) oil and toss.

Meanwhile, toast pine nuts in dry large heavy frypan over medium heat for 3 to 5 minutes or until golden, stirring and shaking pan frequently. Remove from pan and set aside.

Add remaining 1 tablespoon (15 mL) oil and butter to frypan and increase heat to medium-high. Add chard stalks, onion, garlic and dried red pepper; saute for 4 minutes or until tender. Add chard leaves and stock; cover and cook for 3 to 4 minutes or until tender, stirring occasionally. Add salt and pepper to taste.

Add chard mixture, pine nuts and ¼ cup (50 mL) parmesan cheese to pasta; toss. Transfer to serving platter. Sprinkle with remaining cheese. ♺

WHAT IS SWISS CHARD?

If you like beets and spinach, you'll like swiss chard. This cousin of the beet has crinkly green leaves that are tender and tart. The celery-like stalks (also edible) can be white, red, even yellow. As with beets, the red colour can bleed on to other ingredients. Cook the leaves like spinach, with just the water that clings after washing. The stalks can also be eaten — trim and discard any tough portions then chop stalks across the grain; cook a little longer than the leaves.

TIPS

• Pine nuts can be toasted in the oven. Spread on rimmed baking sheet and bake at 325 F (160 C) for 6 to 8 minutes or until golden.

• Buy pine nuts from stores that have a fast turnover — these nuts can go rancid quickly. Store pine nuts in an airtight container in the refrigerator for up to 2 months, or for up to 9 months in the freezer.

Per serving:

463 calories, 18.2 g protein, 19 g fat, 57.4 g carbohydrate. Excellent source of vitamin A, thiamin, riboflavin and niacin. Excellent source of magnesium. High in fibre.

Broccoli, Mushroom and Goat Cheese Fettuccine

Makes 4 servings

Broccoli and cauliflower, both cruciferous vegetables rich in antioxidants, provide crunchy contrast to soft mushrooms and creamy sauce in this easy pasta dish. The goat cheese behaves like a luxurious light cream sauce, but with a more complex and inviting flavour. For a fresh, citrus counterpoint, add a butter lettuce salad with orange slices and diced red onion.

¾	**pound (350 g) fettuccine**
2	**cups (500 mL) small cauliflower florets**
3	**cups (750 mL) small broccoli florets**
½	**(14 g) package dried porcini mushrooms**
1	**tablespoon (15 mL) olive oil**
1	**onion, chopped**
2	**garlic cloves, minced**
3	**cups (750 mL) thinly sliced button mushrooms (about ½ pound/250 g)**
½	**teaspoon (2 mL) dried basil leaves**
½	**teaspoon (2 mL) dried thyme leaves**
	Pinch dried crushed hot red pepper
¼	**cup (50 mL) vegetable stock or pasta water**
⅓	**cup (75 mL) unripened soft goat cheese**
	Salt and pepper

Cook fettuccine in large pot of boiling salted water until tender, adding cauliflower for the last 3 minutes of pasta cooking time and broccoli for the last 2 minutes; drain and return pasta and vegetables to pot.

Meanwhile, in small microwaveable bowl, combine dried mushrooms and ½ cup (125 mL) water. Microwave on High for 2 minutes; strain through sieve set over bowl. Coarsely chop soaked mushrooms; return to bowl with mushroom liquid and set aside.

In large heavy frypan, heat oil over medium-high heat. Add onion, garlic, button mushrooms, basil, thyme and dried red pepper; saute for 7 minutes or until mushrooms are golden.

Reduce heat to low; add stock, soaked mushrooms with their liquid, and goat cheese, stirring until cheese melts. Add sauce to pasta and vegetables; toss. Add salt and pepper to taste. Transfer to serving platter. ↻

TIME SAVER: Purchase washed, ready-to-use fresh broccoli and cauliflower: A 340 gram package yields 3 cups (750 mL) broccoli and 2 cups (500 mL) cauliflower.

SUBSTITUTION: Dried mushrooms deliver a rich, earthy flavour. Try using dried shiitakes or chanterelles instead of porcini. Dried mushrooms are available in the produce section of most supermarkets.

Per serving:

499 calories, 19.6 g protein, 11 g fat, 82.1 g carbohydrate. Excellent source of vitamin C, riboflavin, niacin and folate. Excellent source of magnesium, phosphorus and zinc. High in fibre.

Perogies with Tomato-Basil Sauce

Makes 4 servings

As much as we love the taste of butter or sour cream spooned over perogies, those toppings pack mega-calories. But change the sauce, and the dish is kinder to the waistline. Want proof? Check the fat and calorie counts below. These are perogies for the health-conscious, with plenty of flavour from the tomato-basil sauce and a sprinkling of parmesan. Round out the meal with green beans, sauteed with garlic and lemon zest.

1	(796 mL) can diced tomatoes, drained
3	tablespoons (45 mL) olive oil
4	garlic cloves, minced
¼	cup (50 mL) chopped fresh basil or 1 teaspoon (5 mL) dried basil leaves
½	teaspoon (2 mL) salt
1	(1 kg) package frozen potato and cheddar cheese perogies
¼	cup (50 mL) grated parmesan cheese

In large heavy saucepan, combine diced tomatoes, oil, garlic, basil and salt. Bring to a boil over medium-high heat; reduce heat and simmer for 12 minutes.

Add perogies to large pot of boiling salted water; return to a boil and cook for 2 minutes or until perogies float. Drain and add perogies to the sauce; stir to mix. Transfer to serving platter. Sprinkle with parmesan cheese. ⟳

WHAT ARE PEROGIES?

Perogies are little bundles of flavour — in this case, pasta wrapped around a potato-and-cheese filling, but there are many other taste combinations available. Depending on your mood, choose from a variety of fillings: cheddar cheese, cottage cheese and potato-and-onion, to name just a few.

Per serving:

606 calories, 17.7 g protein, 17.9 g fat, 95.8 g carbohydrate. Excellent source of calcium, magnesium, phosphorus and zinc. High in fibre.

SUBSTITUTION: If you can't find fusilli lunghi, substitute any other long-strand pasta: spaghetti, fettuccine, linguine or tagliatelle.

Per serving:

514 calories, 16.8 g protein, 14 g fat, 80 g carbohydrate. Excellent source of riboflavin, niacin and folate. Excellent source of magnesium, phosphorus and zinc. High in fibre.

Fusilli Lunghi with a Whole Lotta Funghi

Makes 4 servings

Fusilli lunghi looks like spaghetti with a corkscrew perm. Here the strands are entwined with three kinds of mushrooms: button, oyster and shiitake. This is definitely a dish for mushroom-lovers. The long pasta strands give the fork and the mushrooms a little something to grab on to. To complete the meal, set out a platter of cooked young green beans dressed in extra-virgin olive oil and a splash of balsamic or sherry vinegar.

¾	pound (350 g) fusilli lunghi (long curly pasta)
3	tablespoons (45 mL) olive oil
1	small onion, cut into thin wedges
1	garlic clove, minced
3	cups (750 mL) thickly sliced button mushrooms (about ½ pound/250 g)
2¼	cups (550 mL) thickly sliced oyster mushrooms (about ¼ pound/125 g)
2	cups (500 mL) thickly sliced, stemmed shiitake mushrooms (about ¼ pound/125 g)
¾	cup (175 mL) vegetable stock
¼	cup (50 mL) dry white wine
4	plum tomatoes, chopped
2	tablespoons (30 mL) chopped fresh tarragon
½	teaspoon (2 mL) salt
½	teaspoon (2 mL) pepper
¼	cup (50 mL) grated parmesan cheese

Cook fusilli lunghi in large pot of boiling salted water until tender; drain and return to pot.

Meanwhile, heat oil in large heavy frypan over medium-high heat. Add onion and saute for 3 minutes or until onion is tender. Add garlic, and button, oyster and shiitake mushrooms; increase heat to high and saute for 4 minutes or until tender. Add stock, wine, tomatoes, tarragon, salt and pepper; cook for 3 minutes, stirring occasionally.

Add sauce to pasta and toss. Transfer to serving platter. Sprinkle with parmesan cheese. ◔

Spanish Tortilla

Makes 4 servings

In Spain, tortilla has a meaning that's different from what the word conveys in North America — it's an omelette that is sliced, like a quesadilla, into wedges. Suffice to say, it's made with eggs and it's simple and lovely. It can be served tapas style, but in larger portions makes a great meal. If you're watching our 30-minute limit on prep and cooking time, this one's a squeaker because the potatoes won't be rushed. Serve with toasted rustic bread and tomato slices.

¼	**cup (50 mL) olive oil**
2	**pounds (1 kg) red potatoes, peeled and sliced very thin**
1	**small onion, sliced very thin**
3	**garlic cloves, minced**
	Salt and pepper
6	**large eggs**
1	**tablespoon (15 mL) chopped fresh rosemary**
¼	**cup (50 mL) grated parmesan cheese**
	Chopped fresh parsley

In 12-inch (30 cm) heavy nonstick frypan, heat oil over medium heat. Layer potatoes, onion and garlic in frypan, seasoning each layer with salt and pepper. Cover and cook for 15 minutes or until potatoes are tender, turning once.

In large bowl, whisk together eggs, rosemary, and ¼ teaspoon (1 mL) each of salt and pepper.

Pour egg mixture over potatoes; cook for 5 to 6 minutes or until bottom is golden, lifting the edges of tortilla with spatula and tilting pan occasionally to allow uncooked egg to run underneath. Loosen tortilla; slide on to pizza pan. Invert pan, returning tortilla, cooked side up, to frypan. Sprinkle with parmesan cheese and cook for 3 minutes or until eggs are fully set.

Cut tortilla into wedges; sprinkle with parsley. ⏱

TIP: Don't be tempted by the convenience of store-bought dried or bottled minced garlic — it lacks the intense flavour of the real thing, freshly minced.

Per serving:

428 calories, 17.3 g protein, 20.8 g fat, 44.2 g carbohydrate. Excellent source of vitamins B6, B12, riboflavin, niacin and folate. Excellent source of magnesium and phosphorus. High in fibre.

TIP: French omelettes can be tricky and time-consuming when making several at once, but the Italian equivalent, frittata, is much more forgiving. It doesn't need to be folded like a French omelette, so it's easier to make. One (10-inch/25 cm) frittata can serve 4 comfortably.

Per serving:

398 calories, 18.5 g protein, 16.5 g fat, 44.2 g carbohydrate. Excellent source of vitamins B12, C, thiamin and folate. Excellent source of iron and phosphorus.

Mushroom Frittata in Pita Pockets

Makes 4 servings (2 pita halves per serving)

Go ahead — eat your frittata with your hands. Here the flavourful egg mixture is tucked into a pita pocket with tomato, lettuce and salsa. Suddenly, the dependable, hard-working frittata becomes almost festive.

6	**large eggs**
2	**tablespoons (30 mL) milk**
	Salt and pepper
1	**tablespoon (15 mL) chopped fresh basil**
2	**tablespoons (30 mL) olive oil**
½	**small sweet onion, chopped**
2	**garlic cloves, minced**
1½	**cups (375 mL) chopped, stemmed shiitake mushrooms (about ¼ pound/125 g)**
½	**small red bell pepper, chopped**
2	**tablespoons (30 mL) grated parmesan cheese**
4	**(7-inch/18 cm) pita breads, cut crosswise in half**
8	**thin slices tomato**
	Shredded lettuce
	Salsa

In large bowl, whisk together eggs, milk, ½ teaspoon (2 mL) salt and ¼ teaspoon (1 mL) pepper until frothy. Whisk in basil and set aside.

Preheat broiler.

In 10-inch (25 cm) heavy ovenproof frypan, heat oil over medium heat. Add onion and garlic; saute for 30 seconds. Add mushrooms and red pepper; saute for 3 minutes or until vegetables are tender. Spread mixture evenly over bottom of frypan. Reduce heat to medium-low and remove frypan from heat.

Stir egg mixture and pour into frypan over vegetables. Return frypan to heat and cook for 5 to 7 minutes or until frittata is almost set, lifting edges of frittata and tilting pan occasionally to allow uncooked egg to run underneath.

Sprinkle frittata with parmesan cheese and broil for 1 to 2 minutes or until top is puffy and golden. Lightly sprinkle with salt and pepper to taste. Cut into 8 wedges.

Place 1 wedge of frittata in each pita half with a slice of tomato and lettuce. Top with a dollop of salsa. ↺

Asparagus and Goat Cheese Frittata

Makes 4 servings

Asparagus and goat cheese are calming soul-mates. Here they elevate a simple frittata to elegant status. Unlike traditional omelettes, which are made one serving at a time, the multi-serving frittata is a one-pan affair. Cut into wedges, add a green salad, and you have a light spring dinner.

½	pound (250 g) asparagus, trimmed
6	large eggs
2	tablespoons (30 mL) milk
½	teaspoon (2 mL) salt
¼	teaspoon (1 mL) pepper
½	cup (125 mL) unripened soft goat cheese, cut into small pieces
1½	tablespoons (22 mL) vegetable oil
½	small onion, chopped
1	garlic clove, minced
1	small red bell pepper, chopped
1	small tomato, seeded and chopped
2	tablespoons (30 mL) grated parmesan cheese

Bring large frypan of salted water to a boil over medium-high heat. Add asparagus and cook for 2 to 3 minutes or until tender-crisp. Drain and pat dry with paper towel. Cut asparagus into 1-inch (2.5 cm) pieces.

Meanwhile, whisk together eggs, milk, salt and pepper in large bowl until frothy. Stir in goat cheese and set aside.

Preheat broiler.

In 10-inch (25 cm) heavy ovenproof frypan, heat oil over medium heat. Add onion, garlic and red pepper; saute for 3 minutes or until onion is tender. Stir in asparagus and tomato; spread mixture evenly over bottom of frypan. Reduce heat to medium-low and remove frypan from heat.

Stir egg mixture and pour into frypan over asparagus mixture. Return frypan to heat and cook for 5 to 7 minutes or until frittata is almost set, lifting edges of frittata and tilting pan occasionally to allow uncooked egg to run underneath.

Sprinkle frittata with parmesan cheese and broil for 1 to 2 minutes or until top is puffy and golden. Cut into wedges and serve. ⟲

ASPARAGUS IS A SNAP TO PREPARE

Size is a matter of preference: Some like thin stalks, others prefer them thicker. Whichever you favour, choose crisp asparagus with tight tips (budding indicates the asparagus is old).

To remove tough ends of asparagus, hold centre of stalk with one hand, and root end of stalk with your other; bend asparagus until it snaps at the point where it gives most easily. Discard the tough end.

There is no need to peel asparagus nowadays, unless you have purchased large, mature spears that may have tough fibrous skin and large scales.

Store spears in the fridge: Stand them up in a container with about 1 inch (2.5 cm) of cold water, then cover loosely with a plastic bag. Alternatively, wrap asparagus in a damp towel inside a plastic bag for up to 3 days.

TIP: Purchase about ¼ pound (125 g) unripened soft goat cheese to yield about ½ cup (125 mL).

Per serving:

648 calories, 28.5 g protein, 21 g fat, 93.9 g carbohydrate. Excellent source of vitamins C and B12. Excellent source of calcium and magnesium.

 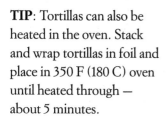
Scrambled Egg and Tomato Fajitas

Makes 8 fajitas (2 per serving)

TIP: Tortillas can also be heated in the oven. Stack and wrap tortillas in foil and place in 350 F (180 C) oven until heated through — about 5 minutes.

Scrambled eggs are so basic and so simple that sometimes they need an imaginative lift. Here's what can happen when you free your mind and do more with them. Mushroom scrambled eggs wrapped in a tortilla with some cheese, tomato, salsa and greens make a wicked combo. Serve with a salad of baby greens and chopped avocado.

8	large eggs
2	tablespoons (30 mL) milk
1	tablespoon (15 mL) thinly sliced green onion
¼	teaspoon (1 mL) salt
⅛	teaspoon (0.5 mL) pepper
1	tablespoon (15 mL) vegetable oil
1	cup (250 mL) thinly sliced mushrooms (about 3 ounces/85 g)
8	(8-inch/20 cm) flour tortillas
½	cup (125 mL) grated gruyere or cheddar cheese
½	cup (125 mL) mild salsa
8	thin slices tomato
2	cups (500 mL) lightly packed fresh baby spinach or shredded lettuce
	Mild salsa for garnish, optional

In large bowl, lightly whisk together eggs, milk, green onion, salt and pepper; set aside.

Meanwhile, in large heavy nonstick frypan, heat oil over medium-high heat. Add mushrooms; saute for 2 minutes or until tender. Reduce heat to medium and add egg mixture; cook for 3 to 4 minutes or until set, stirring frequently.

Stack and wrap tortillas in paper towel; microwave on High for 30 to 40 seconds or until heated through.

For each fajita: Place ⅛ of the egg mixture in centre of 1 warmed tortilla. Sprinkle with 1 tablespoon (15 mL) cheese, then top with 1 tablespoon (15 mL) salsa, 1 slice of tomato and ¼ cup (50 mL) spinach.

Fold bottom of tortilla (side closest to you) up over filling; then fold sides in, overlapping. Top with additional salsa, if desired. ⏱

Per serving:

492 calories, 24.4 g protein, 23.6 g fat, 48.3 g carbohydrate. Excellent source of vitamins A, B12, thiamin, riboflavin, niacin and folate. Excellent source of calcium, magnesium and phosphorus. High in fibre.

Black Bean and Pepper Wraps

Makes 4 servings

Tortilla wraps allow you to make a one-handed meal that can include something as messy as black beans. A little heat from jalapeno pepper, sweetness from red bell pepper and the freshness of lettuce and salsa combine in this sassy Latin handful. If you can't find 12-inch tortillas, use more 10-inch ones, with less filling in each. If you want to make the meal cutlery-free, serve with fruit kebabs for dessert.

1	tablespoon (15 mL) vegetable oil
1	onion, chopped
1	jalapeno pepper, chopped fine
2	garlic cloves, minced
1	small red bell pepper, chopped
1	(540 mL) can black beans, drained and rinsed
½	teaspoon (2 mL) salt
¼	teaspoon (1 mL) pepper
4	(12-inch/30 cm) whole-wheat tortillas
4	tablespoons (60 mL) chopped tomato
4	tablespoons (60 mL) medium salsa
1⅓	cups (325 mL) shredded lettuce
4	tablespoons (60 mL) light sour cream

In large heavy frypan, heat oil over medium-high heat. Add onion, jalapeno pepper and garlic; saute for 2 minutes. Add red pepper and saute for 2 minutes. Add beans and mash coarsely with fork; cook for 1 to 2 minutes or until heated through. Stir in salt and pepper.

Stack and wrap tortillas in paper towel; microwave on High for 30 to 40 seconds or until heated through.

For each wrap: Place 1 tortilla on work surface. Put about ¾ cup (175 mL) bean mixture on bottom half of tortilla (side closest to you) and mound in an oblong (about 5 inches/13 cm by 2½ inches/6 cm) about 3 inches (7 cm) from bottom of tortilla and 2½ inches (6 cm) from sides. Top bean mixture with 1 tablespoon (15 mL) tomato, 1 tablespoon (15 mL) salsa, ⅓ cup (75 mL) lettuce and 1 tablespoon (15 mL) sour cream.

Bring bottom edge of tortilla (side closest to you) up over filling. Fold sides in toward centre. Roll up to form a rectangular package. ⏂

HOT ZONE

Much of a chili pepper's heat lies in its raised ribs. There lurks capsaicin, the colourless irritant that produces the burning sensation. The seeds are the second hottest part of a pepper — cut out both, and most of the fire is gone.

Per serving:

267 calories, 12.9 g protein, 6.5 g fat, 41.6 g carbohydrate. Excellent source of vitamin C, thiamin and folate. Excellent source of iron and magnesium. Very high in fibre.

EXTRA FAST

WHAT ARE BOCCONCINI?

Although these "little mouthfuls" of fresh mozzarella were once made from the milk of Italian water buffalo, today most North American versions are made from cow's milk. These small misshapened balls of fresh white cheese can be found in Italian delis or supermarkets. Store this very mild cheese in the refrigerator, submerged in enough water to cover, and use promptly.

The Caprese Panino
Makes 4 servings

We liked the Caprese Panino at Tony's Deli on Commercial Drive in Vancouver, so we asked for the recipe. The popular lunch spot obliged. The idea for the sandwich comes, of course, from the classic Italian caprese salad of fresh bocconcini, tomato and basil. A good quality baguette is critical to success. The only addition this meal needs is a refreshing beverage — perhaps a sparkling Italian soda? For dessert, feast on a platter of grapes and thin wedges of ripe red bartlett pear.

1	baguette (20 inches/50 cm long and 3½ inches/9 cm wide)
¼	cup (50 mL) basil pesto
12	large fresh basil leaves
3	balls bocconcini (fresh mozzarella), about ½ pound (250 g) total
2	plum tomatoes, sliced thin
2	tablespoons (30 mL) thinly sliced, drained sun-dried tomatoes (packed in oil)
	Salt and cracked pepper
1	teaspoon (5 mL) balsamic vinegar
1	teaspoon (5 mL) extra-virgin olive oil

On cutting board, cut baguette lengthwise, almost in half, leaving one long side joined. Spread pesto over cut surface.

Line the entire length of one half of the bread with single layer of basil leaves. Cut bocconcini balls in half, then cut each half into ½-inch (1 cm) thick slices. Place cheese slices, in single layer, on top of basil leaves, followed by tomato slices. Sprinkle with sun-dried tomatoes, and salt and pepper to taste. Drizzle vinegar and oil over top of fillings.

Place sandwich on rimmed baking sheet and bake at 350 F (180 C) for 8 to 10 minutes or until cheese has melted slightly. To serve, cut crosswise into 4 equal pieces.

Per serving:

517 calories, 21.8 g protein, 28.9 g fat, 43.3 g carbohydrate. Excellent source of vitamin B12 and niacin. Excellent source of calcium and phosphorus.

Burritos Without the Beef

Makes 8 burritos (2 per serving)

When mixed into a thick tomato sauce, soy-based "ground round" makes a far more convincing substitute for beef than, say, a soy burger. Not one of our tasters was able to tell that this was not what it seemed: ground beef. Vegetarians along with die-hard meat eaters will enjoy this recipe.

1	tablespoon (15 mL) vegetable oil
1	onion, chopped
2	garlic cloves, minced
1	(398 mL) can diced tomatoes
1¼	cups (300 mL) mild salsa, divided
1	small green bell pepper, chopped
1	large plum tomato, chopped
1	(340 g) package Mexican-flavour Veggie Ground Round, crumbled
	Salt and pepper
8	(8-inch/20 cm) flour tortillas
1	cup (250 mL) grated blend of 3 cheeses (cheddar, monterey jack and mozzarella)
2	cups (500 mL) shredded lettuce
½	cup (125 mL) chopped fresh cilantro
½	cup (125 mL) light sour cream

In large heavy saucepan, heat oil over medium-high heat. Add onion and garlic; saute for 3 minutes or until tender. Add canned tomatoes, ¾ cup (175 mL) salsa and green pepper; bring to a boil. Reduce heat and simmer for 5 minutes. Add plum tomato and simmer for 5 minutes or until most of the liquid has evaporated. Add Veggie Ground Round, and salt and pepper to taste; heat through for 1 minute.

Stack and wrap tortillas in paper towel; microwave on High for 30 to 40 seconds or until heated through.

For each burrito: Spoon about ½ cup (125 mL) plus 2 tablespoons (30 mL) ground round mixture in mound across the bottom half of tortilla (side closest to you). Sprinkle with 2 tablespoons (30 mL) cheese blend, ¼ cup (50 mL) lettuce and 1 tablespoon (15 mL) cilantro. Bring bottom edge of tortilla (side closest to you) up over filling and roll up to enclose filling. Serve with remaining salsa and sour cream. ○

TIPS

- Mexican-flavour Veggie Ground Round is well seasoned, but if you like fiery hot food, serve burritos with a medium or hot salsa.

- Tortillas can also be heated in the oven. Stack and wrap tortillas in foil and place in 350 F (180 C) oven until heated through — about 5 minutes.

Per serving:

590 calories, 35.8 g protein, 25.2 g fat, 62.7 g carbohydrate. Excellent source of vitamins A, B12, C, thiamin, riboflavin and folate. Excellent source of iron, zinc, magnesium and phosphorus. Very high in fibre.

Pop-'Em-in-the-Oven Quesadillas

Makes 8 quesadillas (2 per serving)

In the race to the dinner table, this recipe is jet-propelled. You mix the filling, encase it in tortillas, pop 'em in the oven for about 10 minutes, and the Mexican-inspired quesadillas are ready to eat. While canned olives are tolerable, far better to seek out the more intense ones sold in brine by Italian and Greek grocers. Round out the meal with a big bowlful of crisp salad greens drizzled with your favourite vinaigrette.

2	cups (500 mL) chopped seeded tomatoes (about 2 large)
⅓	cup (75 mL) chopped onion
¼	cup (50 mL) chopped pitted black olives
2	tablespoons (30 mL) chopped fresh cilantro or parsley
1	tablespoon (15 mL) lime juice
8	(8-inch/20 cm) flour tortillas
2	cups (500 mL) Tex-Mex grated cheese (a blend of mozzarella, cheddar and monterey jack with jalapeno) Vegetable oil

In medium bowl, combine tomatoes, onion, olives, cilantro and lime juice.

For each quesadilla: Place 1 tortilla on baking sheet. Spread with about 5 tablespoons (75 mL) tomato mixture and sprinkle evenly with ¼ cup (50 mL) Tex-Mex cheese. Fold tortilla in half and brush lightly with oil.

Bake quesadillas at 425 F (220 C) for 8 to 10 minutes or until cheese is melted. ⟳

TIP: To seed a tomato, cut in half horizontally, then use a spoon to remove seeds and pulp. Alternatively, gently squeeze in one hand to remove seeds and pulp.

Per serving:

485 calories, 20.3 g protein, 25.9 g fat, 46.1 g carbohydrate. Excellent source of thiamin and riboflavin. Excellent source of calcium and phosphorus.

Quick Pizza Dough

Makes two 12-inch (30 cm) pizza crusts

It may not seem possible, but it's true: Using instant yeast and a food processor, you can make a chewy, satisfying pizza crust that's kneaded for one minute and needs only a 10-minute rest before it's ready to put in the oven.

For each of our oven-baked pizzas, you have the option of using either this Quick Pizza Dough recipe or prebaked commercial pizza crusts for your base. If you use the store-bought crusts, put toppings on and place on pizza pan. Bake at 450 F (230 C) for about 10 minutes. If using home-made pizza dough, put toppings on and bake at 500 F (260 C) for 8 minutes, then slide pizzas from pan directly on to oven rack and bake for an additional one to two minutes or until bottoms of crusts are crisp and golden.

4	cups (1 L) all-purpose flour
2	(8 g) packages instant yeast
2	teaspoons (10 mL) salt
1	teaspoon (5 mL) granulated sugar
	Water
2	teaspoons (10 mL) olive oil

In large-capacity food processor fitted with steel blade, combine flour, yeast, salt and sugar. Heat 1½ cups (375 mL) water and oil until hot to the touch, 125 to 130 F (50 to 55 C). With motor running, gradually pour hot water mixture through feed tube. Process, adding up to 2 tablespoons (30 mL) cold water, until dough forms a ball, then process for 1 minute to knead.

Turn dough out on to lightly floured surface, cover with plastic wrap and let rest for 10 minutes.

Divide dough in half. Roll out each piece on lightly floured surface to form 12-inch (30 cm) circle. Place each in 12-inch (30 cm) pizza pan.

TIP: You can freeze this pizza dough. Let dough rest for 10 minutes, then divide in half and flatten each piece into a disc about 6 inches (15 cm) in diameter. Freeze each disc in greased plastic freezer bag for up to 1 month. Thaw at room temperature for about 4 hours, or in refrigerator for about 8 hours.

Per pizza crust:

1,130 calories, 30.7 g protein, 7.5 g fat, 229 g carbohydrate.

Black Bean Pizza with Salsa and Onion

Makes 4 to 6 servings

Time-saving products help preserve the sanity of most everyday cooks. With an assist from already grated cheeses, bought salsa, canned black beans and prebaked crusts, this pizza can be ready in about 15 minutes. Quicker than take-out or delivery, wouldn't you say? This was a hit with our tasters.

- ⅔ cup (150 mL) mild salsa
- 2 (12-inch/30 cm) purchased, prebaked thin pizza crusts
- 1 cup (250 mL) finely grated part-skim mozzarella cheese
- 1 (398 mL) can black beans, drained and rinsed
- 2 garlic cloves, minced
- 3 plum tomatoes, sliced thin
- 2 cups (500 mL) finely grated Nachos & Tacos cheese (a blend of 6 cheeses)
- 2 tablespoons (30 mL) chopped green onion
- 2 tablespoons (30 mL) coarsely chopped fresh cilantro

For each pizza: Spread ⅓ cup (75 mL) salsa evenly over pizza crust leaving 1-inch (2.5 cm) border. Sprinkle with ½ cup (125 mL) mozzarella cheese. Top with half the beans, garlic and tomatoes. Sprinkle with 1 cup (250 mL) Nachos & Tacos cheese.

Bake at 450 F (230 C) for 8 to 10 minutes or until cheese is melted and toppings are hot. Sprinkle each pizza with half the green onion and cilantro. ○

TIP: All the cheeses used in this recipe are sold grated in handy, resealable packages. The Nachos & Tacos blend includes pepperjack, cheddar, monterey jack, queso quesadilla, queso blanco and asadero. If you can't find that mixture, create your own blend using monterey jack, cheddar and pepperjack.

Per serving:

907 calories, 42.3 g protein, 25.9 g fat, 125 g carbohydrate. Excellent source of vitamin B12, thiamin, riboflavin, niacin and folate. Excellent source of iron, zinc, magnesium and phosphorus. Very high in fibre.

Tomato-Pesto Pizza with Two Cheeses

Makes 4 to 6 servings

Many green herbs have been used to make variations on classic pesto, but one of our favourites isn't green — it's bright red. Intensely flavourful sun-dried tomato pesto is a kitchen treasure (store it in the fridge). For this pizza, rather than use traditional tomato sauce, we start with a thin layer of the tomato pesto, then add two cheeses, garlic, olives and basil. The sky's the limit.

4	tablespoons (60 mL) sun-dried tomato pesto
2	(12-inch/30 cm) purchased, prebaked thin pizza crusts
2½	cups (625 mL) grated provolone cheese
½	cup (125 mL) thinly sliced red onion
2	garlic cloves, minced
4	plum tomatoes, sliced thin
½	cup (125 mL) pitted black olives, halved
½	cup (125 mL) grated asiago cheese
½	cup (125 mL) shredded fresh basil
	Pepper

For each pizza: Spread 2 tablespoons (30 mL) pesto over pizza crust, leaving 1-inch (2.5 cm) border. Sprinkle with ¾ cup (175 mL) provolone cheese. Top with half the onion, garlic, tomatoes, olives and asiago cheese. Sprinkle with ½ cup (125 mL) provolone cheese.

Bake at 450 F (230 C) for 8 to 10 minutes or until cheese is melted and toppings are hot. Sprinkle each pizza with half the basil. Sprinkle lightly with pepper.

TIP: Once sun-dried tomatoes became popular, bottled and refrigerated sun-dried tomato pesto quickly followed. A little goes a long way — the intense, assertive flavour adds a quick boost to pizzas, sandwiches or vegetables.

Per serving:

866 calories, 37 g protein, 29.7 g fat, 111 g carbohydrate. Excellent source of vitamin B12, thiamin, riboflavin and niacin. Excellent source of calcium, iron and phosphorus. Very high in fibre.

Olive, Mushroom and Grape-Tomato Pizza

Makes 4 to 6 servings

WHAT ARE GRAPE TOMATOES?

These red (and sometimes yellow or orange) tomatoes, as the name implies, are about the size and shape of large grapes. They can be pricey, but they're also sweet and juicy — great for snacking.

TIME SAVER: Buy crumbled seasoned feta cheese in resealable plastic bags or tubs. It comes in several flavour combinations — we like one with oregano, cracked peppercorns and sun-dried tomatoes.

SUBSTITUTION: Use regular crumbled feta cheese instead of the seasoned version; the flavour will be a little tamer.

Per serving:

802 calories, 30.4 g protein, 26.3 g fat, 110 g carbohydrate. Excellent source of vitamin B12, thiamin, riboflavin, niacin and folate. Excellent source of calcium, magnesium and phosphorus. Very high in fibre.

Tomatoes the shape of grapes are among summer's fine treats, and they're increasingly available at other times of the year. Cut in half and sprinkled along with black olives on a pizza crust, they look like edible polka-dots. Add mushrooms and mozzarella, then a scattering of pine nuts and feta cheese, and the result is a rich and flavourful pizza. Accompany these warm pizza slices with a quick caesar salad. Simply combine crisp, torn, romaine lettuce with a couple of chopped anchovy fillets, crunchy croutons and a good grating of parmesan cheese, then drizzle with bottled caesar dressing.

2	(12-inch/30 cm) purchased, prebaked thin pizza crusts
3	teaspoons (15 mL) olive oil
2	cups (500 mL) grated mozzarella cheese
½	small red onion, sliced thin
1½	cups (375 mL) sliced mushrooms (about 4½ ounces/130 g)
¼	cup (50 mL) pitted kalamata olives, halved
1	cup (250 mL) grape or cherry tomatoes, halved
½	cup (125 mL) crumbled seasoned feta cheese
1	large garlic clove, slivered fine
2	tablespoons (30 mL) pine nuts
	Pepper
2	tablespoons (30 mL) shredded fresh basil

For each pizza: Lightly brush pizza crust with 1½ teaspoons (7 mL) oil, leaving ½-inch (1 cm) border. Sprinkle with ½ cup (125 mL) mozzarella cheese. Arrange half the onion and ¾ cup (175 mL) mushrooms on top. Top with half the olives and tomatoes (cut side up). Sprinkle with ¼ cup (50 mL) feta cheese, half the garlic and 1 tablespoon (15 mL) pine nuts. Sprinkle with ½ cup (125 mL) mozzarella cheese.

Bake at 450 F (230 C) for 10 minutes or until cheese is melted and toppings are hot. Sprinkle with pepper to taste and 1 tablespoon (15 mL) basil.

Pear and Brie Pizza

Makes 4 to 6 servings

This excellent pairing was inspired by Tuscany Pizza on Bowen Island, near Vancouver. The pizzeria has a wood-fired oven and we don't, but however it's baked, the result is delicious. Starting with the pear and brie, we've added pecans, caramelized onions and thyme. Bring on your demanding and sophisticated palates. Make a brief stop at the deli to pick up some grilled vegetables to complete the meal.

2	sweet onions (about 1 pound/500 g total)
1	tablespoon (15 mL) butter
2	tablespoons (30 mL) olive oil, divided
2	tablespoons (30 mL) balsamic vinegar
	Salt and pepper
2	(12-inch/30 cm) purchased, prebaked thin pizza crusts
¼	pound (125 g) brie cheese, cut into small pieces
¼	cup (50 mL) pecans, chopped coarse
1	large pear, cored, peeled and sliced thin
1	teaspoon (5 mL) fresh thyme leaves
	Watercress sprigs

Cut onions in half lengthwise; then cut each half crosswise into thin slices (you should have about 3 cups/750 mL).

In large heavy frypan, heat butter and 1 tablespoon (15 mL) oil over medium heat. Add onions; reduce heat to medium-low and saute for 15 minutes or until tender, stirring frequently. Stir in vinegar and saute for 3 minutes or until onions are very tender, stirring frequently. Add salt and pepper to taste.

For each pizza: Brush pizza crust with 1½ teaspoons (7 mL) oil, leaving ½-inch (1 cm) border. Spread with half the caramelized onions. Top with half the brie cheese and pecans. Arrange half the pear slices on top.

Bake at 450 F (230 C) for 10 to 12 minutes or until cheese is melted and toppings are hot. Sprinkle each pizza with half the thyme and garnish with watercress. Sprinkle with salt and pepper to taste. ◐

TIP: Watercress is usually eaten raw in salads or sandwiches, or cooked in soups and other dishes. But it also makes an attractive, flavourful garnish— the dime-size green leaves have a distinctive peppery flavour. Store in the refrigerator in one of two ways: upright, with the stems in a glass of water and all covered loosely with a plastic bag, or wrapped loosely in paper towel and placed in a plastic bag.

Per serving:

851 calories, 23.9 g protein, 24.8 g fat, 132 g carbohydrate. Excellent source of vitamin B12, thiamin, riboflavin, niacin and folate. Excellent source of phosphorus. Very high in fibre.

Individual Grilled Asparagus Pizzas

Makes 4 servings

With a prepared pizza crust in hand, the possibilities are endless, so use a combo such as this one as a starting point. This mixture of grilled asparagus, yellow pepper and onions keeps moist and flavourful under the melted Italian cheeses. Serve with a platter of cut fresh vegetables and store-bought dip such as baba ghanoush (a Middle Eastern puree of eggplant, tahini, olive oil, lemon juice and garlic).

½	**pound (250 g) asparagus, trimmed**
	Purchased olive oil flavoured with garlic
4	**(6-inch/15 cm) purchased, prebaked pizza crusts**
2	**cups (500 mL) grated Italian cheese mix (a blend of mozzarella, provolone, parmesan and fontina)**
¼	**sweet onion, sliced thin**
½	**small yellow bell pepper, chopped**
	Pepper
4	**tablespoons (60 mL) shredded fresh basil**

Brush asparagus with garlic oil and place on barbecue grill over medium-high heat. Cook for 8 minutes or until almost tender, turning occasionally. Remove from grill and let cool slightly. Reduce heat to low.

While asparagus is cooking, start to assemble pizzas. Sprinkle each pizza crust evenly with ¼ cup (50 mL) cheese mix. Top each with a quarter of the onion and yellow pepper.

Cut asparagus into 1-inch (2.5 cm) pieces and divide evenly among the crusts. Sprinkle each with ¼ cup (50 mL) cheese mix.

Place pizzas on grill over low heat and close lid. Cook for 6 to 7 minutes or until cheese is melted and toppings are hot. Remove from grill and sprinkle each pizza with pepper to taste and 1 tablespoon (15 mL) basil. ♂

Per serving:

738 calories, 33.8 g protein, 22.3 g fat, 99.4 g carbohydrate. Excellent source of vitamins A, C, B12, thiamin, riboflavin, niacin and folate. Excellent source of calcium, iron, zinc, magnesium and phosphorus. Very high in fibre.

Tex-Mex Cheese Fondue

Makes 4 servings

A fondue is a communal process where hearts, minds and forks converge over the cooking pot, so consider making this for the family on a night when they aren't rushing off in all directions. The alcohol in the beer will evaporate during cooking, so you can serve this to children. Use some creativity in choosing the dippers — try steamed asparagus, broccoli, cauliflower and halved new potatoes. And you can't go wrong with unsalted taco chips for the kids.

3	cups (750 mL) finely grated gruyere cheese (about 6 ounces/170 g)
2	cups (500 mL) coarsely grated monterey jack cheese flavoured with jalapenos (about 6 ounces/170 g)
1	tablespoon (15 mL) all-purpose flour
¾	cup (175 mL) beer
1	tablespoon (15 mL) lime juice
1	garlic clove, minced
1	green onion, chopped fine
¼	cup (50 mL) coarsely chopped fresh cilantro
1	baguette, cut into 1½-inch (4 cm) chunks (about 8 cups/2 L)

In medium bowl, combine gruyere and monterey jack cheeses. Sprinkle with flour and toss to coat; set aside.

In large heavy saucepan, combine beer, lime juice and garlic. Place over medium heat and bring to a simmer. Reduce heat to low. Gradually add cheese mixture, stirring constantly until cheese is completely melted. Transfer to fondue pot; set over fondue burner. Sprinkle with green onion and cilantro. Serve immediately.

To serve, place bread chunks in basket. Spear bread chunk with fondue fork and dip into melted cheese; remove from fork into small bowl and eat with regular fork. ⏱

TIP: If your cheese fondue is too thick, stir in a little warm beer to thin it out.

Per serving:

497 calories, 27.8 g protein, 28 g fat, 29.8 g carbohydrate. Excellent source of vitamin B12 and niacin. Excellent source of calcium and phosphorus.

INDEX

(Boldface type denotes recipe by its full name)

S

TIP INDEX